The Diary Of A Former Sex Addict

by:
PORSCHE DAY
Thick Nubian Goddess

ISBN: 978-0-578-80118-6

Ordering Information: *For information about special discounts available for bulk purchases, sales promotions, fund-raising and educational needs, contact the Author at the above email.*

I would like to dedicate the first of many books

*to my daughter **Zena-Marie Gordon**.*

Mommy loves you.

I would like to give Special Thanks to Alecia Brown, Aaron Clark, Jasmine Day, C.J. Harris, OGW Publishing (Odessa), and many others that have been there for me through my journey of building my brand and writing my book.

PROLOGUE

I don't remember the exact date. I'm just trying my hardest to let it all out like the doctor said…...

I remember hearing Daddy yelling at Brenda saying that he never wanted him here!

'How could you lie to me Brenda? Are you high?"

All the nights I cried silently. I feared for my life.

All I could hear was him blaming me for this.

He said that I wanted this to happen. That he noticed the way I looked at him…but I barely looked at him! I don't even know him!!!

When he came to our house to live Daddy was at work. It was before winter break was over for school. Brenda took off and

Grandma Mabel as usual was at home sitting in that stinking rocking chair.

Brenda says " hug your Uncle Todd kids!" We all went to hug him and it felt as if he hugged me extra tight. Later that day he barged in on me in the bathroom. I was so mad that he saw me naked in the tub. Brenda says he just got home from being in the service. But Daddy found out that was all a big lie. Daddy barely speaks to him though. I thought he would be happy to see him since he never met him before but he was not.

I tried to stay close to Little John and Vanessa every time Uncle Todd came in from work, wherever that was.

One night Little John spent the night out and Vanessa was sleeping in the bed with me. He came in and raped me quickly. He made me stand up and do it. Brenda wasn't home as usual and Daddy was at work. I hate her! She only cares *about herself and her damn drugs! Vanessa stayed asleep the entire time.*

He says "Don't it feel good Tiffy?" As he grabbed my wrist. "Yes." I was lying of course. Why would anyone want this?

I was able to cover my bruises because it was winter. Once it got hotter. He would rape and hurt me in ways nobody could see.He would pull my hair! It's not like anyone would believe me anyway if I told them.

Daddy stayed home all day one time. I was safe and Uncle Todd never once came out his room. I don't even think he came out to use the bathroom. Daddy and I had a great day too. We went to the Gallery Downtown. Daddy brought me, Little John, and Vanessa sneakers. We ate at McDonalds too. Daddy asked how we were doing. I wanted to tell him what was happening to me. But then I thought what if Daddy thinks I'm fast like Brenda. I didn't say a word, I just had fun with my Daddy that day.

August 1, 1995 is a day that I'll never forget. KYW news time was 10:42 it was another hot day 95 degrees with humidity at 90%.

Oh great! That means I gotta stay on the porch! Let me hurry up and get dressed before he wakes up I thought to myself as I started to head outside.

"Tiffy, were you leaving out before giving Unc his sugar?" I heard him see. I was too late.

"I was hurrying to go play with-" my sentence was interrupted.

He already pulled down his pants and pinned me down to the bed. I knew not to scream or he would choke me again. I wish I was dead!!! Maybe I should scream so he could choke me so hard that I never wake up I thought!!!

Pop!!!!!!!

His heavy body fell on top of me. I could taste his blood in my mouth. I pushed him off of me not sure what had happened. It was Daddy. He saved me! The look on my Daddy face was scary. I never seen Daddy look like this before. Am I next? Does Daddy think I wanted to do this?

I replay this day at least a million times before sleep when I wake up. Why did this have to be my life?

August 1, 1995

John

Something ain't right. I don't want to think the worst but I know something is going on.I feel it in my gut.Every since he's been in the house I couldn't shake this feeling.

John lit up his cigarette and started pacing. He had circled the block of his job six times. He decided to tell his boss he couldn't finish his shift today. He got back in his car and looked at his gun, a black Smith & Wesson 9 millimeter. John started getting carried away with his thoughts as he drove back home.

I know the other two children ain't mine. I don't care what that bitch says!!! I love them, it's not their fault she's a whore. All the stories about her messing around on me. It's even stories about her and my own cousin! I know the boy got to be his...I know it. All I ever did was be a good man. I had a chance to be somebody...but she trapped me with Tiffany. I was preparing to be drafted to play pro ball overseas. They will understand later John thought to himself. Tiffany that's my daughter and I must protect her! I'm gonna kill him that's it! John's thoughts were all over the place.

John and Brenda had been together since ninth grade. John was the 'good guy' and Brenda was the 'troubled girl'. John played basketball since sixth grade and became a local star. Brenda was the cute light skin girl. Brenda was short with long hair. They met in math class. Brenda pretended to need help with algebra just to get John's attention. At the time John's girlfriend was Lisa. Brenda started showing up to John's basketball practices. She would stare at John so much that Lisa became jealous. *"I'm just her math torture."* John would explain to Lisa. *"Naw she's trying to take you away from me. She barely comes to class but she never misses your practices!"* Lisa one time caused a major scene that got John detention so he couldn't torture Brenda that day. Brenda was always on some slick shit. She hated school and hated being at home even more. Her mission in school was to be that bitch. Brenda wanted to be the 'It' girl. She had taken many of her classmates' boyfriends just because she knew that she could. Some of the girls were supposed to be her friends. Brenda had no friends except Joy. Joy was just as ruthless as Brenda. They would jump girls never to give a fair one and would barely catch one without the other. Their nickname was BJ that's how tight they were. John was attracted to Brenda's rude and selfish ways. A part of him thought he could change her. Brenda was his first. He had the perfect fairytale life planned out for them. John was offered to play overseas ball as a freshman in college. Brenda didn't go to college. After high school she begged John not to leave her for Penn State. Brenda knew what she had to do something so she stopped taking her birth control pills. I remember the night she took her mother's car to drive up to see me play. Brenda looked so beautiful she had on the promise ring I had given her. We won that game against Temple. I scored 40 points. I was the man!!! Brenda and I celebrated hard that night but she seemed just a little bit off. She was actually paying attention to me. That night in the dorm was the first time we made love in a bed. We didn't start having sex until twelfth grade and when we did it was in my uncles van. He had an idea of what was going on but he never said anything. Uncle Doug... John thought. But Brenda had already been around the block. That night in my dorm is how we made Tiffany. My parents were so disappointed with me. My Mama won't even see me. All she ever said to me was that Brenda was no good. Divine...aw man I don't even want to remember that. Why didn't you stay with Lisa? Why didn't I? Lisa is now a doctor and moved to California last I heard. I allowed Brenda to waste my time and life. I have nothing else to lose.

He drove home with his mind made up.

When John arrived his mother in law was sitting in her rocking chair watching Jerry Springer. John looks at his house that he allowed to fall apart. The once beautiful three bedroom row home he purchased in southwest philly, a few blocks away from Cobbs Creek has gone to shit. Every time he would save up some money to get the house fixed up Brenda would do something outrageous and he would have to bail her out of jail for some bar fight. Or she owed money to the corner boys from buying cocaine. Telling them to get it from my husband he will be home around 8 tonight was her favorite line. Look at who I have become, John thought. I'm thirty one. I'm still young. I should be in my prime and traveling the world. Jail has got to be better than this hell! Married to this scandalous ass whore! I was good to her! I was almost in on being a firefighter and she took that from me! Every time I would get back on my feet Brenda would bring me down. It's cause she knew, she knew once I got it together I was leaving her! I was gonna take my children and go! I love those children. I don't know who Little John Daddy is but I know Vanessa is Derricks. My own first cousin. The rage was consuming John.

"John, what are you doing home early?" Grandma Mabel was startled to see him.

John did not respond, he went straight upstairs, he heard the radio in the kids room and he thought he heard the bed squeak. He takes out the gun before opening the door. He opened the door and saw his brother in law on top of his sweet innocent baby girl. John shot Todd immediately in the back of the head.

Mabel was shakened...was that a gunshot?

She turned down the chants of 'Jerry Jerry Jerry'

She hears Tiffany crying and runs up the stairs to find her only son laying down on Tiffany's bed with his pants down and a single gunshot wound to the back of the head. She grabbed her chest. "No no no you killed my boy!" John is holding Tiffany, he gets up and points the gun at Mabel.

"I should kill you too!" Then he points the gun to himself. "I should kill myself for not seeing sooner! I knew I should've taken my children away from here!" John begins mumbling to himself holding the gun at his side.

Tiffany is in the corner rocking back and forth. Mabel faints....someone called the police.

Brenda

"Girl I'm sick of John's ass!" Brenda expresses to her best friend Joy.

"Yeah right!!! He is still sleeping in the basement?" Joy asked as she decided to take the next customer.

"Uh huh I'm not giving him nothin'! No food and no coochie" Brenda exclaims while counting out money for her customer. The middle aged woman just stared at her with disgust.

"What?" Brenda states popping her gum

"I can't wait to get off! I'm not closing either! I'm going home changing and seeing Robert ha!" Brenda snaps her finger as she happily explains that she is cheating on her husband. Joy and Brenda were laughing as Pat came rushing in cutting in front of everyone in line at the check cashing place.

"Brenda!!!! You have to leave now!!! It's Tiffany."

"What about her little fast ass now!"

"It's John! John killed Todd!" Pat cried uncontrollably and began to shake.

Brenda runs from behind the glass and grabs Pat.

"What the hell are you talking about? You're lying!"

"We...have to go," Pat manages to say.

Joy can't believe what she heard but she couldn't leave her post. John killed Todd she thought to herself as a smirk appeared followed by the words; Good.

The Hospital

"Tiffany is going to be ok. We are going to do a rape kit on her the Doctor explained to Brenda.

"What are you saying Doctor? She wasn't raped!" Brenda shouted.

"Mrs. Brown-" the Doctor was immediately interrupted by Brenda.

"I'm not trying to hear shit you talking about!" Brenda starts crying and kicking the wall.

Pat walks out the room with the doctor leaving Brenda to her anguish.

"Doctor, was my niece raped?"

"Yes. According to Tiffany and her vagina does have tears consistent with forced entry." Pat breaks down after receiving confirmation from the Doctor. The Doctor is rubbing Pat's shoulder consoling her as she wept for her niece. A nurse comes and whispers in the Doctors ear.

"The police are inside the room now questioning Tiffany."

Pat asked if she could come in and the Doctor informed her she would be able to go in shortly. Pat waits outside the room.

Tiffany is laying in her hospital bed looking at the two detectives. She is nervous and anxious about what they are about to ask her. Will I get in trouble too? She thought. Will they believe me? Where's Daddy? Tears start flowing down her face. The short Hispanic female detective hands her a tissue.

"Tiffany, I'm Detective Garcia. We are not here to hurt you. This is my partner Detective Thompson."

"Where is my Daddy? Is Uncle Todd dead for sure?

Where is Brenda?" The Detectives both looked at each other.

"Your Father is in police custody. Your Uncle is dead. Your Mother is in the hallway. Would you like for me to get her?"

"No keep that crazy bitch away from me! I told Dr. Howard what happened and all I know!" Tiffany throws the hospital blankets over her head.

" We understand we need to hear it from you. You stated your Uncle has been sexually abusing you."

"Yes! No one would believe me! Because of that time at school. Kevin told that big lie about me..." Tiffany's mind drifted back to the day in seventh grade. It was the day before spring break and everyone was in the school yard during breakfast. Tiffany rushed out the house before Uncle Todd could get up that morning. She wanted to see Janell and tell her the plan she had come up with. Tiffany wanted to run away. While she was sitting on her book bag impatiently waiting for Janell Kevin walked up and approached her. He was so cute but he got on my damn nerves! Tiffany thought to herself. "Tiffany I know you think I'm cute and you alright so you wanna come over to the bushes with me? Kevin stated confidently" Tiffany looked at him and smiled. She got up and rolled her neck and eyes with the reply of "hell no!"

"Forget you Tiffany!" Kevin said as he walked off. Janell came up to Tiffany with a penny candy bag. "What did Kevin want?" Janell asked, a little surprised and excited. Kevin was in the top ten of the cutest boys in the seventh grade Janell thought. He was brown skin, tall, and had an athletic build. "He ain't want nothing but to get on my damn nerves. He asked me to go with him to the bushes." Tiffany stood up and grabbed her book bag. "You ain't go?" Janell looked puzzled. "No, I told you I have a plan. I'm not worried about no damn Kevin!"

Later on in school all the boys were smiling and grinning at Tiffany. Even fat boy Tommy whose only joy is food smiled and said "hello." Tiffany didn't think about it too much. She figured it was because she sprayed some of her mother's bath and body work perfume on that morning. I smell good, they all wanna speak, Tiffany thought. Rhonda, Kevin's girlfriend came up to Tiffany in the hallway with a group of girls.

"You fuckin' my man?" Rhonda asked Tiffany as she began to put her hair in a ponytail. Tiffany looked puzzled. "What?!? No, don't nobody want him!"

"That's not what I heard! Kevin telling everybody how you and him were in the bushes this morning!"

The other girls all nodded their heads yes in unison. Tiffany dropped her book bag. She knew it was only one way out of this. She grabbed Rhonda by the neck and slammed her into the lockers. "Ain't nobody messing with Kevin!" Rhonda grabbed Tiffany's hair and they both fell to the floor. Tiffany began punching Rhonda in the face. As soon as Rhonda's friends saw Tiffany was winning they jumped in. Janell instantly came to Tiffany defense also. Tiffany's older cousin Keke, an eighth grader, showed up to help protect her younger cousin. One of Keke's friends went to get her out of art class when she observed the unfair fight. Security finally came and broke the fight up. All you could hear from the students were screams and laughter.

All the girls involved in the fight were placed in two different offices. Tiffany sat next to Janell who had an ice pack over her head, one of the girls had kicked her in the head. "Thanks for having my back Nell. I'm gonna get Kevin fucked up!" Tiffany states to Janell. All the parents were called to pick up their children immediately. "Keke where did you come from?" Tiffany asked. "Art." They all burst out laughing.

Brenda, Pat, and Janell's grandmother walk in to collect the girls. Brenda jumped immediately on Tiffany. "They told me you're out here with boys in the bushes!" Brenda grabs Tiffany by the hair.

Pat grabs Brenda. "Chill! What do you want the cops to come lock us up next? Damn." "I didn't touch him!" Tiffany explained. "I know ya fast ass did! You think I don't know you fuckin? My birth control pills have gone missing."

Tiffany thought to herself yeah I'm having sex alright! I'm being raped and if I tell on him he will kill me.

Tiffany thought about Brenda's words to her on the entire ride home in Aunt Pat's minivan. Tiffany truly despised Brenda. She wanted to tell it all but she knew no one would believe me. Just because Brenda was a hoe of her time don't mean Tiffany wanted to follow in her footsteps.

I just wanted to run away, Tiffany thought. I don't want to be here anymore. Tiffany stared out the window with tears coming down her eyes. Why is this my life? Why can't I be like Janell and have normal parents? Janell is going to Disney World for Spring Break. Cousin Keke house is nice and clean and I'm just lucky if Uncle Todd can't come out of his room because Daddy's home. Which isn't too often because Daddy was always working. Life wasn't fair.

Keke already knew she wasn't in much trouble; she was protecting her cousin. Pat was a different kind of mom. She didn't want to make the same mistakes as Grandma. Whatever they were. Grandma seemed fine to Keke, but it's not like she saw her much. Keke looked out the window content with being suspended for three days.

"Tiffany...Tiffany what big lie?" Detective Garcia asked. Tiffany took the blankets from over her head. "That I did it to him in the bushes."

Detective Thompson shook his head and started writing. Tiffany explains to the Detectives that her Uncle moved in earlier that year after being released from the halfway house.

She explained how her father didn't want him there. The Detectives left out the room and explained to Pat that they will have to come down to the district and give a full statement. Pat agreed and told the police she will have Tiffany and Brenda there as soon as possible.

Pat walked back down the hall to Brenda who appeared to have calmed down.

"Brenda tell me you had no idea of what Todd was doing to Tiffany?"

"Hold up you think our brother would rape her fast ass? Brenda asked."

Pat looks at Brenda with disgust. How is she my sister?

"Are you kidding me Brenda! You know what he has been accused of before! He was in jail for raping an underage girl! Have you forgotten about Tanya's daughter? Tiffany just turned 13 in July! The same age as Tanya's girl. Todd raped her! I'm taking Tiffany!"

A security guard interrupted Pat rant to tell them to keep it down or they will be escorted out of the hospital. Brenda walked up to Pat and whispered to her "None of it is true! You understand me bitch? You're not taking my daughter." Brenda walked away and left Children's Hospital. Pat looked at her niece and nephew who sat in the waiting area with tears flowing down their eyes. Vanessa and Little John are Tiffany's siblings. Little John is only two years younger than Tiffany. "Where's Mommy and Daddy?" Vanessa cries.

She hugged both of them. "Everything will be ok."

Pat took them home with her for the night because she knew Brenda was going to be missing.

Brenda

Brenda took the El train to see Robert. He was waiting for her at their favorite spot, a little no name bar. Brenda knew Robert would have her lines of cocaine waiting. Brenda went right in snorting the coke using her lucky dollar. Brenda then demanded straight shots of E&J. Fuck all of them, Brenda thought. Todd is gone…John killed my brother! He will rot in jail for this. My mother is at Misericordia. Hell naw I'm not gonna let them fuck up my high Brenda thought as she tried to calm the voices inside her head.

"Hey baby got anymore coke?" Robert lays out another line. "Baby you feeling alright? I got word that-"

"Shhh…let's go." Brenda commanded Robert before he could start in with all his questions. That was the last thing she wanted to hear was what somebody had told him about today.

They left the bar and went back to Robert's place. Robert lived in a shabby apartment on top of a corner store in southwest philly. Brenda and Robert had history. When John worked overnight securing the docks Brenda was having an affair with Robert. Brenda suspected that Robert was her son's father. She never received a DNA test to confirm this. John accepted him and never asked questions. He just wanted to be under the illusion that his wife wasn't as fucked up as everyone says. Brenda had not seen Robert in years; he was locked up for some fraud shit. She didn't know exactly what he did and didn't care. Brenda knew he had her fix and do-able dick.

Once they entered the apartment Robert put on his stereo to the 'Quiet Storm' on radio station Power 99. Brenda immediately started undressing. Cocaine really did a number on her once coke bottle shape. But that didn't stop the show. The best head giver in town she named herself. Robert wasn't much of a looker anymore either. He was a high school football legend. He lost all his muscle tone but gained a beer belly. Brenda pulled out Roberts semi hard penis and started sucking on it like her life depended on it. Robert started moaning and shaking, he had to sit down on the bed. Brenda got on top of him and started riding him hard. They looked like two sticks creating a fire.

Tiffany

During her stay at Children's Hospital of Philadelphia Tiffany attended individual and group therapy. Pat spoke with the doctors. The Doctor instructed Pat to give Tiffany more time to heal. Brenda didn't care anymore; she decided she didn't want Tiffany in the house. Tiffany's therapist; Dr. Stacy gave her a composition book and a pretty fluffy blue pen. "If you don't want to talk to me, talk to your dairy. Tell your story. Write it all Tiffany it will help you release the pain." Tiffany looked at her and the composition book. "Will this really help me? I mean you want me to tell my story? So you can read it and tell me?" Tiffany asked. "No I won't read it but one day you may look back and see how far you have come." Dr. Stacy pointed out. Tiffany wasn't fond of the children there. Some of them were straight weirdos. Some of the kids were rich and wanted problems. Dallas is faking for attention

Tiffany thought as she started to think about the other children in the program. Dallas was from some suburb. Her parents wanted her to have the best treatment. All she did was yell, kick, and scream. They need to beat her ass Tiffany thought to herself. Uppity black folks as her Grandma Mabel would have called them. Only one that was cool was Mark. Mark didn't talk during the group either. We both would just sit in the back staring at all the other fools. Now this therapist is giving me this journal. Saying it's gonna help me. This pen is cute though Tiffany thought.

For my birthday last month Aunt Pat took me and Keke to see 'Clueless'. They had cute pens like that. Maybe I'll start writing in this journal tomorrow and see if it really helps.

Mark came up to Tiffany at group therapy. "I'm gonna be going home soon Mark said." Tiffany nodded at him. Mark didn't talk much so for him to say anything to her made her feel secretly special. Mark didn't look like the kind of boy who should be in here. Tiffany often wondered what his story was. I mean why would this fine ass boy be in here? He looked so perfect. He was brown skin and tall. Mark had the prettiest curly black hair and a mustache. He has got to be in high school.

Mark sat next to Tiffany on his last night at Children's Hospital. Tiffany smiled the entire session. She even said 'hi' to the other children in the group. After the group Mark walked Tiffany back to her room. "I'm Mark." Tiffany smiled. "I know."

"This was my third time having to stay here but I'm finally getting adopted by my Uncle." Mark explained. "They put you in here for getting adopted?"

"No. I sometimes have a problem but I'm better now. Im gonna play ball for the NBA!" Mark performed a shot with an imaginary basketball. Tiffany laughed. "How old are you?"

Tiffany asked. "I'm about to be fifteen in September. When do you get out of here?"

"I don't know. I think soon." Tiffany replied.

"I'm from West but I'm gonna be moving to South Philly to live with my Uncle. Call me when you get out." Mark wrote his number down on a piece of paper he took from his journal. Tiffany giggled and took the paper happily. That night Tiffany looked at her journal and decided to write her entry:

' I don't know if I'm doing this right but here it goes. Uncle Todd started raping me about two weeks after he moved in. I stayed home from school. I had a stomach ache. Brenda and Daddy were at work. Grandma Mabel as always was downstairs on her rocking chair. He came into my room while I was laying down. He told me to be quiet...I asked him what he was talking about? His pants were down and his thang was out. I got scared..I asked him not to do it. Uncle Todd told me that I was a bad girl. He had been watching me and he* *knew I wanted this. He pinned me down and I screamed but he wrapped his hands around my neck until I passed out. When I woke up my vagina was hurting really bad. I got up to go to the bathroom and saw blood when I wiped myself.'* Tiffany started crying until she fell asleep and she couldn't finish the journal entry.

She dreamed it was her mother shot by her father that night instead of Todd. Tiffany woke up in a cold sweat. Damn do I hate her that much? She got and went to the bathroom. Tiffany could hear her roommate Jennifer talking in her sleep. 'Please stop Daddy! Please stop...' Jennifer kept saying in her sleep. "I can't wait to get out of here!" Tiffany whispered to herself.

Tiffany was released from the hospital. She stayed with her Aunt Pat and Uncle Jake. They lived on a nice block called Cedar Avenue by Misericordia Hospital. Pat kept Vanessa and

Little John the night before but Brenda came over raising hell to give her back her children. Brenda told Pat " You can keep that bitch Tiffany!" Vanessa and Little John were happy to see their mother.

"Where's Daddy?" Asked Vanessa

"In jail where he belongs!" Brenda screamed and threw both children in Hack man Ricky's station wagon. Tiffany watched from the upstairs window in Keke's room. Keke had her own room and tv. Her twin brothers share a room with bunk beds. I had to share a room with Vanessa and Little John, Tiffany thought. We all had to share one bed. Often nights I would just sleep on the floor. Vanessa would pee the bed sometimes. Brenda would expect me to wake her up to make sure she goes to the bathroom. I'm not her damn mother Tiffany thought to herself. Grandma Mabel had given her room to Uncle Todd. That's when Daddy really had it with Brenda and

Grandma both. He wanted Uncle Todd to stay in the basement. He really didn't want Todd to come at all.

Uncle Jake is a firefighter for the City of Philadelphia. Aunt Pat stays home and raises the children. I know Brenda is jealous of that. Brenda is jealous of Aunt Pat because her daddy took care of her. Brenda and Uncle Todd's dad was killed over a dice game down the bottom Grandma said.

I remembered Uncle Jake wanted Daddy to be a firefighter too but he failed due to his knee injury. Brenda stabbed him with a knife in the right knee. We were all downstairs with Grandma. Daddy came home late. Brenda was pregnant with Vanessa. I was eight and little John was six. "Where the fuck you been?" Brenda asked John holding a kitchen knife. "Brenda hold on now...I told you I was taking Paul shift tonight we need the money."

Brenda started walking up on John. " You are lying! You fuckin' around on me? Huh?" Brenda knew damn well she was the one fucking around. That she was pregnant with Derrick's child, John's first cousin. John has barely touched her since he caught her in bed with Toya. She swears no one knows that she goes both ways. Toya was ugly to me. She had real short hair and was fat. She tried to sound like a man. Telling Brenda that me and Little John would move with her down south. Yuck lady. I remember that night Daddy caught them in the bedroom. Daddy came home early from overnight work. I heard him coming up the stairs so I waited to open my bedroom door. The next thing I heard was "Who the fuck is this?" Daddy yelled. I opened my door to peek and I saw ugly ass Toya come out the room in men's boxers. Tiffany chuckled to herself. She goes back to thinking of the night her father was robbed of a promising future.

John started backing up into the porch door but Brenda ran up on him and was aiming for his balls but he threw his right knee over them and Brenda stabbed him deep in the knee.

John screamed and pushed Brenda down. Tiffany ran in the kitchen and got paper towels. She put them over her father's knee. Little John started crying. Grandma Mabel just sat in her rocking chair. Rocking back and forth. Brenda got up from the hardwood floor and called the police immediately. "I'm pregnant and you put your hands on me!" John didn't respond; he had passed out. His big break from becoming a firefighter was over. That is the day Tiffany truly started hating her Mother. Blood was all over the floor. The Judge threw the whole case out in family court. Daddy had to go to physical therapy for months because of Brenda.

Keke stared at Tiffany wondering what she was thinking about. "Tiffany, what are you thinking about?"

"Nothing. We gonna listen to Monica?" Keke threw on the tape. The girls sat on the white carpet listening to Monica and reading Goosebumps till bedtime.

The next morning Aunt Pat called Brenda on the phone. It took forever for someone to finally pick up. "Hello." Mabel answers. "Hello Mom is Brenda there?"

"Yes but she doesn't want to talk to you." Mabel explained. "Mom we have to go to the police station-"

"You believe that bitch Tiffany?"

Aunt Pat was not surprised at the response she was getting from her mother. Mabel can't stand Aunt Pat. Aunt Pat was raised by her father Nathan and his wife Carol. Mabel only had visitation rights to Aunt Pat. "Mabel you know Tiffany can't be making it up. She wasn't even born when Todd was locked up!"

"That's enough out of you Patricia! You can take her to cops yo self ya hear me! Always trying to break up the family!" Mabel hung up on Aunt Pat. Aunt Pat slammed the phone down. Damn it! Shit! I'm glad my father didn't allow me to be raised by her. She's a horrible mother. She never wanted to admit that Todd was a rapist. He raped his girlfriend's daughter while she was pregnant with his child. The horrific deed caused Todd's ex-girlfriend to lose her child while trying to commit suicide. I was there the entire trail. He was sentenced fifteen years but was released for 'good behavior'. Todd even went to counseling while in the halfway house as part of his release. Mabel put up her house for Todd. Aunt Pat pulled herself together and called Tiffany down to the kitchen. Tiffany came down and sat down at the table. Something her kitchen didn't have. Brenda sold their kitchen set when she went cocaine benching.

"Yes Aunt Pat?"

"We gotta go to the station without your mother."

Tiffany rolled her chinky brown eyes. Why am I not surprised?

"Okay, but I want to see my dad also."

"Once we go to the station and sort things out. I'll take you to see John. I promise. God only knows what he's going through." Aunt Pat began fixing breakfast. "Aunt Pat, why aren't you like my mom? I mean you believe me." Tiffany asked with tears flowing down her eyes. "I believe you because I know the truth about Todd so does everyone else. They want to live in denial. I told your father why Todd was in jail before he got out to warn him."

Tiffany was surprised. That explains why Dad put up a fuss about him coming to live with us. I thought he just didn't like Uncle Todd.

"So Daddy didn't know that Uncle Todd was a rapist the whole time?"

"No. Brenda lied and said Todd was coming home from the service. She and I got into a nasty fight when she found out I told John the truth. She probably blames me too for Todd's death."

Tiffany got up from the table and hugged her Aunt.

"Thank you. I wanted to die but instead my daddy saved me, but you helped him try to protect me."

Pat turned around and hugged Tiffany back. Poor John. Poor Tiffany. I just wanted to save them both from Brenda and Mabel. I know I'm in for a fight with Brenda but I will be damned if I abandon my niece Pat thought.

Tiffany and Aunt Pat sat in Detective Garcia's office waiting for her to return. Tiffany was offered a can of Pepsi. She happily drank. She was happy to get it all of her chest. Aunt Pat sat there playing in her jumbo braids. Detective Garcia came back in and explained that Tiffany would have to testify. Pat and Tiffany both agreed. "Can my dad come home? He's not the bad guy! He saved me." Tiffany explains to Detective

Garcia. " That will be up to the courts Tiffany but your testimony will help him."

As promised, Pat took Tiffany to see John. Tiffany couldn't wait to see her Dad. Every night since it happened Tiffany would wake up in cold sweats. All she could see when she closed her eyes was Uncle Todd's body falling on her lifeless and tasting his blood in her mouth. My Daddy saved me. He loves me. Even though she had been dreaming repeatedly about Todd she would rather wake up dreaming about his death than to wake up from dreams of being violated. John picked up the phone with joy when he saw Tiffany and Pat. "Daddy!!!" Tiffany just began crying. So did John. Aunt Pat took the phone. "John how are you?"

John wiped his tears and managed to say. "Thank you Pat. I'm fine. I don't care if I spend the rest of my life here just look after my children."

"I'm gonna do my best. Brenda won't let me have the kids just Tiffany." John took a pause as he knew Brenda would put up a fight. Of course she hates our biological child. "I understand."

Tiffany took the phone. "Daddy when are you coming home?"

"I'm not Tiffany. I need you to understand that I did this." John began to cry. Tiffany stared at her father with grief. "But Daddy, why would they keep you in jail for saving me?! He's the bad guy?!??"

"Tiffany, I love you and I would not change my actions not one bit." He put his right hand on the glass. Tiffany did the same.

The whole ride home Tiffany just kept thinking of the good times her and John had. Father and daughter days walking along Cobb Creek. The Mr. Softee Ice cream she would get with the sprinkles.

Pat was also thinking about how she had to explain all this to Jake. She had to register Tiffany to another middle school for eighth grade one closer to the house. I have to get Keke ready for ninth grade. I'm so proud of her getting into Bok. I have a lot to do this week...Pat thought on the ride back home.

When Jake came in that night from his twenty four hour shift the last thing he wanted to hear was about Brenda's loony toon ass. Jake stood behind Pat's decisions when it came to her family. He isn't from the Cosby's Show himself. Jake and Patricia have been friends forever before dating in high school. Jake didn't know that Carol wasn't her biological mother until they started getting serious. Jake didn't want to be like his parents. At a young age since he could remember he lived with his grandmother Trudy, his mother's mother. Jake's parents were placed in jail for armed robbery. He looked at himself and Pat as the 'second chance kids'. They got pregnant in high school with Keke but that didn't stop them from accomplishing anything. Jake loved Pat whole heartedly and their children. He gave them the life they never had and deserved. Jake enjoyed coming home to a clean house and home cooked meal. His Grandma Trudy taught him a man works and a woman tends to the house and children.

After his shower Jake came and sat in the dining room with Pat. She had his plate hot and ready just how Jake liked it. Pat allowed Jake to get settled in with his food before speaking on the elephant in the room. "Baby you know Tiffany gonna be here with us. John's trail is gonna start next week. I have to get Tiffany registered for eighth grade. I wanted all three but Brenda is not having that." Jake wiped his mouth with his napkin. "You do what you gotta do… ok Pat. Tiffany and Keke can share the room. I'll give you the money to buy Tiff a suitable bed. You need money for family court? What's going on with John's family?" Jake asked with concern.

"You know his family disowns him for staying with Brenda. I called Ms. Lily and she said no one could bail him out. However his cousin is gonna represent John for free."

"I don't think he wanted bail based on our last conversation. He called me since he was locked up." JJ came running in the dining room to see his parents. "Daddy! You killed the fires?" JJ asked smiling with his two front teeth missing. Jake grabs JJ and puts him on his lap. "You know it!"

Pat went to the kitchen to get a glass of wine. I need to relax more. "Ok JJ go on up to bed. I'm gonna be home for a few days." Hearing that made Pat feel so relieved. She didn't have to ask the girls to look after the twins while she ran her errands.

Jake continued on his conversation with Pat. "John lost it. He's a broken man Pat. I told him we were gonna raise Tiffany...well ya know the rest ain't his no how. John is a special man cause I'm not sticking around to be with a nut like

Brenda." Pat listened and sipped her Arbor Mist. "That's ya family I know you want what's best for them kids but if Brenda only gives you Tiffany then don't stress over the rest. When they are old enough they can come here if they want. Or DHS will take them and then we can go get them. What kept them kids was John."

Jake was right, Pat thought. She got up from the table and made her way to her sensual husband. She visually took in all of him; big, strong, tall, dark, muscular she started rubbing on her husband's shoulders and kissing his neck. Then Pat stood in front of Jake and untied her gold robe. Jake started massaging Pat's full D cup golden breast. She sat on top of his lap. They kissed passionately. All these years and every time always tops the last. Pat made her way in between Jake's legs sucking his fat stocky penis getting every inch of him wet. Jake moaned so loud. Pat pointed up to the ceiling to remind him not to wake the children. Pat gets up and slides her husband's love inside of her. She rides her husband gently and then speeds up. Jake holds on to Pats hips the entire time. Every time she began stroking going up and down Jake buried his face in her long braids until he finally caves and cums so hard and long. Jake places Pat on the table and opens her legs. Jake kisses Pats thighs and outer lips. He then sticks his two fingers inside her vagina. Pat moans quietly. He pushes his fingers in and out until she feels all her juices dripping down. Jake puts his whole face in his vagina, his home, his wife.

Brenda

Brenda had left Vanessa and Little John with Mabel for three days. She was on her cocaine binge. Brenda stayed with Robert and his friends. The whole time Brenda was with Robert she did lines of coke and had multiple orgies. Two of Roberts friends took turns having anal sex with her. Brenda was so high she didn't even feel the dicks being thrown in her.

Brenda walks into her house to see the children and her mother in front of television watching Maury. Brenda shook her head. It just had to be one of those whose Daddy episodes. Brenda ignored the show. Mabel looked at her as she rocked back and forth in her chair. "Brenda you know Pat came by here and got all of Tiffany's things with Tracy." Mabel reached down in her bra and got out a pack of NewPorts.

Mabel takes out a cigarette and proceeds to light it up. "Grandma Mabel, my teacher said they're bad for you!" Vanessa points out to her Grandmother.

"Hush up! Your teacher doesn't know shit!" Mabel states as she drags her cigarette long and hard.

"So what! I don't want Tiffany's fast ass here!"

" She said something about court too. Making it legal for her to have Tiffany." Brenda rolled her eyes up in her head. Mabel goes in her bra again to give Brenda a card. "Police come by here too. You need to go down to the district. I'm testifying about that piece of shit husband of yours." Mabel states. "You and me both!" Brenda states. The doorbell rings. Brenda yells from the living room ``Who is it?"

"It's Joy!!"

Brenda let's Joy in the house. Joy had not seen Brenda since the murder. Joy was hesitant to see Brenda. A part of Joy was sincerely tired of Brenda. She started to hate Brenda. After years of a one sided friendship Joy had begun only dealing with Brenda at work. Joy had cards and flowers for Brenda and Mabel. She gave her condolences.

"You gonna stay awhile?" Brenda asked.

"No I can't. Jimmy is waiting outside in the car for me." Brenda rolled her eyes and placed the gifts on her fall apart coffee table. Jimmy took Joy away from me. Ever since they got "saved", Brenda thought. Joy hugged Mabel and the children.

"It's good seeing you and let me know when the funeral is." Brenda walked Joy to the door and said their goodbyes.

"Funeral? Who got money for that?" Brenda asked Mabel. Mabel changed the channel to the twelve o' clock news. "Sunny coming up from North Carolina. Once they release the body we're gonna bury my boy." Mabel stared at television wishing to forget this is her life. Tears started coming down Mabel's eyes. "He ain't have to kill him." Mabel sobbed. Brenda sat down on the couch and looked at the flowers. "I know Mama. I hate John! He always just wanted me to himself." Little John looked up from the television. "Mommy why do you hate Dad?"

Brenda looked Little John straight in the face and said "He killed my brother cause he was jealous!"

"Aunt Pat said he raped Tiffany. Is it true?"

"No Little John! They are all liars! You hear me?!?"

Little John shook his head with disgust and left out the door. Little John was old enough to understand when he was being lied to. My mom is a crackhead, he thought. I want to see my Dad and Tiffany. Little John walked down to his friend James' house. Nathan's mother Veronica lets him in with care. " How are you John?" She asks as they both sit on the long black leather sofa. Jax, Veronica's current boyfriend was also sitting on the sofa. Veronica was the sexy single mother. She always had a man to take care of her and James. Little John doesn't know what Jax does but he has to be rich to be seeing Veronica. Everyone else is living the good life but me, John thought. "Not good Ms. Vern. My mom is lying to me about my dad and Tiffany." John and Veronica look to the stairs to watch James come down. "What up Big John!" James exclaims as he gives John a pound. "Nothin' waiting on you!" Veronica got up from the couch and told the two young boys to be careful outside. They agreed and left the house. "Are you ready to meet Skip? He said it's the same as last time." James states to John as they walk towards Willows Avenue. About three months ago James and Little John were approached by a corner boy named 'Skip' to deliver a package in a book bag to North Philly. The boys made fifty dollars a piece each time. Skip was waiting for them with the black school bag. He was a lanky light skin dude with braids. "What up what up lil' niggas?!?" Skip says as he hands John the book bag. "Not a thing!" James says nonchalantly. John puts the black school bag on. They proceed to their route. The boys catch the G bus, El train, and Broad Street Line. John the whole time is thinking of his plans on what he is going to do with his money. John hides his money in a ditch he made in Cobbs Creek. He doesn't want to draw attention to himself at home. If Brenda had any clue what he was doing she would take his money for sure. After the boys did their drop and received the fifty dollars they parted ways and went home.

Brenda as usual wasn't home. Grandma Mabel was in the living room with a man that John had never seen before. "Baby this is your Uncle Sunny. This is Grandma's brother." John looked at the big man sitting on the flowered loveseat. He does kind of look like Grandma, Little John thought. Sunny was a big man, big muscle arms, big stomach, and big head.

"How are you doing boy?" Uncle Sunny asked. "Fine." Little John answered. "Where is Nessa?" Little John asked Mabel.

"She is upstairs sleeping. Ya mom stepped out."

"Yup." John went upstairs to see his baby sister sleeping. He sat down on the foot of the bed. "I gotta get out." John says to himself. I'm not gonna be like these people. My dad is in jail and my mom is a crackhead whore! We share one bed! One bed! John gets up from the bed to take a shower. He hears his mother in her room on the phone. I thought she stepped out. I guess Grandma Mabel is losing it. "Trail starts Monday and I hope they lock his ass up foreva!!! Fuck him and Tiffany!" John wonders who she is talking to. However he does not want her to see him ease-dropping so he closes the bathroom door.

Tiffany

"Hello can I speak to Mark?"

"Sure hold on" the caller on the other end stated.

" Yo took you long enough to call me!" Mark said as soon as he picked up the phone.

"Yeah I didn't wanna talk to anyone my Daddy got sentenced today"

"You wanna hang out?"

"Yeah sure…where?"

"Come to my house. Meet me at Broad and Federal St."

"Ok take the Broad street line right?"

"You on it. I'll be waiting at the station for you"

Tiffany couldn't wait to see Mark. A high school boy likes me!
Me!

Keke and the twins were downstairs in the living room playing
with play dough.

"Where are you going?" Keke asked.

"To see Mark." Tiffany says happily.

"Who is Mark?" Keke asked as she smashed pink clay in her
hands.

" A high school boy I met in the hospital."

"You sure Mark ain't crazy?"

"Yeah. Where's Aunt Pat?"

" Oh girl some stuff about Uncle Todd and a funeral."

"Fuck him and that funeral!" Tiffany yelled.

The twins in unison said "Ooo!"

Tiffany left out feeling all over the place. I don't want to go to see a boy thinking about some damn funeral! It was hard enough not being able to go to my Daddy's court date for sentencing today. Testifying was even worse. Of course Brenda and Grandma Mabel told the court my Daddy was a monster. They are the monsters! I told the Judge my Daddy saved me! I begged that they let him come home and take us away from Brenda. Tiffany gathered herself and started thinking of Mark.

He's so cute! I can't believe he likes me! Well I mean it wasn't like there were a lot of black pretty girls to choose from at the hospital. The only other girl was Shamika and she was huge! During the group all she did was eat junk food.

Tiffany saw Mark as soon as she came out the tunnel. He was standing there in a Sixers Jersey and black basketball shorts. He gave her a hug. "How are you?" Mark asked as he took her hand. As the two walked to Marks house Tiffany felt butterflies in her stomach. "I don't know. I just found out my Aunt had to go with my family to Todd 's funeral."

"Todd?"

"My dad killed my uncle Todd...he was raping me!" Tiffany started crying.

Mark hurried Tiffany into his house. He opened the door to the house and showed Tiffany in. He sat Tiffany down on the couch and went to the kitchen to get her some water. Tiffany had stopped crying and took the glass from Mark. So much for a good first date, Tiffany thought to herself as she drank the water. "I didn't want to say all this to you today, I'm sorry."

Mark looked at Tiffany in her chinky light brown eyes and said " Girl we were both in that place for something right?" Tiffany nodded and hugged Mark. They laid on the couch in silence. Tiffany fell asleep in Mark's arms. She felt at peace with Mark.

Mark's Uncle walks in the house and sees the two teenagers cuddled up on the couch. "Hey!" He yells to Mark and Tiffany. Tiffany opens her eyes and sees a big white guy standing in the living room over top of them. "Mark this ya uncle?" She asks as Mark gets up to greet him. "Yeah." Mark stated. "Hey Unc! This is Tiffany we met at the hospital. Remember I told you she would come by."

"Yes, hello Ms. Tiffany. I'm Jacob and yes I'm Mark's white uncle. Haha" Jacob laughs.

"Mark's father was my foster brother. He is gone now." Jacob explained. "Gone?"

Mark answers "My pops died in a car crash. He took me from my mom when I was little. He never said why though."

Jacob ordered the teens some pizza and played cards with them. Jacob was curious to know what Tiffany 's story was. She was such a beautiful girl. "Tiffany, why were you in the hospital with Mark?" Tiffany put her face down. " I was raped. I'm not ready to say the rest." Jacob put his hand on Tiffany's shoulder. "It's ok. Mark from time to time gets into trouble but he is a good kid. Aren't you Mark?"

Mark smirks and replies "Yup".

Mark walked Tiffany to the Broad street line. "My uncle was raised by us. My Grandma and them took him in. I don't know why or where he came from but all my life that's all I know." Mark explained to Tiffany. "You never knew your mom? I wish I never knew mine shit." Before Tiffany went down the stairs Mark hugged Tiffany and held her close. "We're gonna be living large when we grow up. I'm going to the NBA! Call me when you get home ok." Tiffany smiled "I will" Tiffany went down the stairs on cloud nine. When she got home Pat was sitting in the living room waiting for her.

"Hey Aunt Pat, I was at my friend's house."

" I'm aware Keke said a boy, who is Mark?"

"I met him at the hospital. We had an adult home..I gotta call him so they don't worry."

Pat looked at Tiffany. "Go on then come back in here so we can talk."

Tiffany called and spoke with Mark briefly. He was happy to hear from her as if he didn't just spend the day with her. Tiffany sat down on the couch next to her Aunt. " I know you got a lot going on inside that head of yours. I had to respect what your Father asked of me."

" I know that Aunt Pat. How many years did he get?"

"They are giving him twenty five years." Pat hated to say this to her niece. She spared her the parts of her mother's laughter when the Judge ruled John's sentence. Or how Mabel yelled in the courtroom "Thank you Jesus!" The Judge had to demand them to settle down. Pat thought she saw Divine sitting in the corner. No it can't be, Pat thought to herself. She turned back to Tiffany whose eyes were watering and the tears started flowing down her cheeks. Pat tried to hold Tiffany but she got up. "Why were you with my mom and em' at his funeral? Tiffany asked."

"I went to the courthouse and then Uncle Sunny was here . I had to see him. He's paying for Todd's funeral. Tiffany I'm on your side but I have to go to the funeral." Pat explains to Tiffany as she attempts to calm her down. Tiffany lay down flat on the living room floor and closed her eyes. Is this my fault? Did I fuck up my Daddy's life? "Tiffany! Tiffany!" Tiffany refuses to answer her Aunt Pat. All she sees is herself back in that house in the corner of the floor watching her Daddy hold a gun to his head. I still don't know how my daddy knew! Tiffany said.

At least Todd's dead now and he can't hurt you anymore Tiffany. I hate Brenda! "Tiffany! Your brother and sister miss you! They came here by themselves." Pat watches Tiffany's eyes open for the first time since she started talking to her.

"How?" Tiffany asked, still laying flat on the floor. Pat sits by Tiffany on the floor and strokes her hair. "Little John said they walked. They were here for a while but I took them back home before it got dark." Tiffany drifted off to sleep leaving Aunt Pat to reflect on the funeral earlier that day.

The Funeral

Mabel wanted her son's funeral to be inside a church. Luckily cousin Janet on Todd Senior's side of the family was a faithful member of a local church in West Philadelphia. Todd was to be laid to rest in the same cemetery as his father Todd Lawrence Jackson Senior. The whole neighborhood had heard about the murder and the rape allegations against Todd. A couple of churches turned down the funeral. The story made the Daily News and Mabel stood by her son regardless. John killed my boy cold blooded. That damn Tiffany was seducing him, I know she was. Mabel, Brenda, and Pat sat together. Mabel and Brenda cried, screamed, and put on a show. Pat just sat and observed them. Not once did she console them. Pathetic ass bitches, Pat thought. This man was my brother and a filthy rapist. What he did to young girls only getting a bullet to the back of head was mercy. I'm glad you're gone! I spit on your grave! I hate you!

I know they know what you were. Pat was so lost in her thoughts and hatred the funeral was soon over.

Outside the church stood Lily and Divine, John's mother and sister. Mabel tried to ignore their faces while coming down the stairs. "I know you see me Mabel!" Yelled Lily. Brenda hurried down the stairs of the church. As Brenda approaches Lily, Divine punches Brenda in the face. "You ain't running up on my Mama bitch!" Brenda falls to the ground. This isn't Brenda's first run end with Divine. They never liked each other. Divine is John's older sister and she knew Brenda was no good from the guys that she went to highschool with. Brenda was known in West and Southwest Philly for spreading her legs and sucking dick. She hated seeing her little brother pussy whoop by that dirty hood rat. Divine caught Brenda with her boyfriend during her twelfth grade year;

Brenda was in tenth grade. The two were coming from Elmwood skating rink. Divine waited outside for them, she received word from an anonymous caller. When Brenda and Tony came out the skating rink and saw Divine waiting with her girlfriend Journey, Tony ran. Divine snatched Brenda by the hair and two got into a bloody battle. You would think John would leave Brenda right? Wrong! He believed Brenda's story of running into Tony there not that they were on an actual date.

Pat dips to the side of the church. She sees Brenda laid out on the ground and laughs. That's what she gets. Mabel helps Brenda up. Lily and Divine are escorted away by family members. "This ain't the time or place!" Sunny shouted to Lily and Divine. "Fuck y'all we getting DNA on all them kids you dirty bitch! I know where you live. I'm coming for you Brenda!" Divine yells as she enters her black Toyota Camry. Brenda is too stunned to respond. I'm gonna have to stab that bitch, Brenda notes to herself. Joy comes over to Brenda and Mabel to see what happened. "What happened?" As if she didn't see Brenda get dropped. "Bitch snuck me! If she comes by my house and I'm going to stab her!" Joy takes out tissue from her purse so Brenda could wipe her bloody mouth. Joy didn't stay inside for the service she just wanted to make sure Todd was dead. She sat in the car debating on if she wanted to go inside in the first place.

"Come on child so we can properly bury my son!" Mabel starts to cry as she gets in the limousine.

Due to the interruption from Brenda and Divine the burial was short and sweet. Pat didn't ride in the limo with Brenda and Mabel; she didn't want to be phony just because of Todd's funeral. She heard some of the cousins whispering about the murder and Brenda getting punched. This is probably why half these people are even here, just to gossip and talk shit later!

"Thanks for coming, Pat. I know this is not easy for you. Your mother ya know...never mind." Uncle Sunny hugs Pat. "I gotta get home. I'll be in touch." Pat gets in her minivan and drives off.

Tiffany

I'm so happy that Little John and Vanessa are here. The twins chased Vanessa around playing tag while Keke, Tiffany, and Little John sat on the bench having a heart to heart conversation. Keke played in Tiffany's hair. "I believe you Tiffany. Our mom is a fuckin' crackhead." Tiffany and Keke started laughing at Little John's statement. "Crackhead ain't the word!" Tiffany exclaimed. Little John gets up from the bench. "I wanna live with y'all. If not I'm getting my own house." Keke laughs at Little John. " How are you gonna get your own house? We just kids? Ya mom won't let y'all come stay with us!" "Watch Keke! I got a plan." Little John paces back and forth debating on telling them his plans. Naw they're gonna see.

I haven't heard from Mark in like four days. I wanted him to meet my sister and brother. I wonder where he could be? I'm gonna have to just go down south philly after school on Monday. I really don't feel like going to school tomorrow. Hmmm maybe I should play sick? Naw Aunt Pat is gonna baby me the whole time. I wouldn't be able to go anywhere. Later on that night Tiffany goes downstairs to get some water and notices Keke about to open the door to go out. "Where are you going? It's 9?!?" Tiffany states. "To see my man Kevin. He's waiting for me outside at the corner. Shhh he's in the eleventh grade." Keke opens and closes the door lightly. Damn it Mark where are you? Tiffany goes upstairs to their room and cuts on the television. Aunt Pat must be knocked out.

The next morning school went by dumb slow. Tiffany couldn't wait to hop the thirty four trolley. As soon as she got off the Broad Street Line Tiffany headed right to the basketball courts. There's Mark! He was out there on the court doing a whole Jordan move on a boy taller than him. She also noticed the group of girls cheering for him. After he scored Mark ran up to a dark skin girl with long braids and kissed her cheek. Tiffany's whole heart dropped to her stomach. She felt so hot and thought she was about to pass out. No! This isn't happening. Tiffany walked inside the courts and stood in plain sight of Mark. Now let's see what you gonna do, Mark she thought. After the game ended Tiffany watched Mark go to the group of girls and then quickly walked over to her. "Hey Tiff! You see me out there getting' them?" Tiffany looked Mark up and down before answering. "Yeah I saw you out there and I saw you kiss that girl!" Tiffany pushed Mark. "What's up huh? You don't answer my calls and now you're out here kissing on other girls?!?" Mark grabbed Tiffany by the arm. "Girl you not my girlfriend okay?!? Why are you sweating me like this? I do like you though!" Tiffany punched Mark in the chest. "Fuck you! Leave me the hell alone!" Tiffany ran off the courts so fast. "Tiffany! Tiff!" Mark yelled. But Tiffany was gone.

Brenda

Since the funeral Brenda had been on guard for Divine. She was carrying a pocket knife at all times. She won't get the chance to hit me like that again; I will cut that bitch Brenda thought. Since the murder Brenda hasn't been back to work. The check cashing place was gracious enough to give her unemployment. Brenda happily took herself to the welfare office for food stamps and cash assistance. Since John was in jail she was now eligible to receive benefits. "He doesn't want us on welfare. Shit why not? She asked out loud. He always thought he was better than me. I know he wanted to take my kids from me. Now he and Tiffany are gone! The other ones not his anyway. I think Little John is Robert's son but I don't think he would take a DNA test. Hell he ain't seen him since he was a baby. Now that I think of it Robert never asked if Little John was his no how. He's gonna see him today."

Brenda was doing something she had not done in a long time. She was cleaning the house. She even took out some chicken wings to fry. Mabel had gone back down south with Sunny. She wasn't sure if her mother was coming back home. She cooked a marvelous dinner. Fried chicken, baked macaroni and cheese, and collard greens with biscuits. Vanessa sat in the living room watching cartoons with not a care in the world. I don't know where Little John is. That boy ain't been home in hours. I know he's out there running around with that friend of his. They better not be getting in no shit. Brenda goes upstairs to shower and change. She hears the doorbell as soon as she steps out the shower.

"Who is it?"

"It's Rob!" Brenda hurries down the stairs to let him in. Vanessa turns to the couch and sees Robert sitting there. "Who is Mommy? That's not my Daddy! When are you taking me to see Daddy?" Brenda immediately had gotten annoyed. "I'm not taking you no damn where! Go upstairs! Now!"

Vanessa got up from the floor and went upstairs crying. Brenda brings Robert a plate of food with a cup of grape kool aid. "Ain't you gonna eat Bren?" Robert asked, stuffing his face. " Naw you know what I want." Brenda laughs. After Robert finishes eating he goes in his pocket and pulls out a sandwich bag of cocaine. Brenda goes to the refrigerator for her forty she had been saving to go with the coke. Brenda takes her lucky dollar out her bra and rolls it up. Brenda and Robert happily snort up the coke.

Little John walks in the door in the middle of Brenda and Robert's cocaine party.

"What the fuck!" Little John says with his eyes wide with disgust.

"Boy what the fuck did you just say?" Brenda gets up from the couch.

"Who is this man? Why is he here?" John demands.

"None of your Goddamn business!" Brenda is face to face with Little John. Robert looks at Little John and notices the strong resemblance between them. Is he my son Robert thought. Brenda never said her boy could be mine. Play it cool Robert thought to himself. "Maybe I should go Brenda. I could come back later after you feed the kids and get them in bed."

"You ain't welcomed here just cause my daddy locked up don't mean you be a hoe!" Brenda couldn't believe the words that came out of Little John's mouth. Brenda went to slap Little John but he caught her right hand. "I ain't Little John no more! You ain't hitting me either! You fuckin' crackhead!" Brenda backs off. "Get out!!! You think you grown get out of my house!"

"Fuck you Brenda! I hate you! You took my sister and my daddy away!" John walks out the house. I'm never coming back, he said as the door slammed behind him.

Brenda rushes upstairs to check on Vanessa. She is sound asleep. Fuck my high is gone! Robert left me! Brenda lays in her bed and begins to cry.

Pat

It was a beautiful fall day. Pat was getting the twins ready for a day out. She decided to let the boys wear matching outfits today. Jason and Jake are identical twins. Jake is also known as JJ instead of junior since he came out first. At times Pat could not tell them apart. Jason recently fell down the stairs while horseplaying so now he has a cut above his left eye. The phone rings and JJ answers. "Hell-woo?" JJ quickly passes the phone to his mother and leaves the room. "Yes?"

"Is Little John there?" Pat didn't even recognize Brenda's voice; she sounded like she had been crying.

"No, Brenda. What's going on?"

"I kicked him out like a week ago. But now the school is calling here saying he ain't been showing up! I thought he would have come to your house."

"What the hell is wrong with you? You kicked out your eleven year old child? Have you gone to the police?"

"No then DHS is gonna get involved that could mess with my food stamps! Damn don't you know nothing about the system? Shit! Fuck I call you for?" Brenda hangs up on Pat. Pat looks at the phone. Why am I not surprised? Where the hell is that boy? Pat goes to the girls room. Keke and Tiffany are lounging on their beds discussing boys. "Tiffany have you seen or heard from Little John?"

"No. Why?"

"He's missing and Brenda hasn't called the police!" Tiffany got up and started getting dressed. "I'll go check a few friends' houses! He can't be far!" Tiffany started crying and panicking. "Calm down Tiffany. I'll go with you." Keke assures Tiffany everything will be fine.

"So much for a day out with my boys!" Pat states as she gathers the children in the car.

Tiffany

Where the fuck is Little John?!? It's been a month and no one has seen him. The school stopped calling Brenda so he must be going again. .All his friends said they haven't seen him. James' mom Veronica said she would keep a look out for Little John. She claims he spent the night once then told James he was going back home. I know they are lying for him! But why hasn't he come to see me and let me know he's okay.

I need to see my Daddy. I wrote him a letter a few days ago, I can't wait until he gets it! I can't wait until after school tomorrow to go down south Philly to meet Keke. I like high school boys better than the boys in my grade. They take you out to eat and to the movies. They don't have to ask for permission to go out. I love it. I can't wait to see Dawson. He plays on the football team and is in the tenth grade. We did it once so far. Nobody was home at his house. He licked my coochie. I never experienced that before. I had all these clear stuff come out and I felt different. I want to keep feeling that feeling always.

Tiffany laid back on her bed and started rubbing her vagina with her fingers. Keke bursts in the door. Keke falls on her bed and spreads her arms out. She then turns to Tiffany. " I almost had sex! I mean he put it in but it hurt so he took it out!" Tiffany just laughs. Is she for real? "Keke what else are y'all doing? I mean you don't want him to get bored with you." Keke put her head down. "I know I know! The other night he took it out and asked me to suck it! It was so big and curved! I got scared." Tiffany thought about Dawson's penis. His don't curve that's weird. I wonder if something is wrong with her boyfriend. "Girl you better make sure he doesn't have a problem! Dawson's don't do that!" Keke got up from the bed and started undressing to take a bath. Tiffany watched her cousin. She admired her body. Keke had thick thighs and a big breast. All I had was a big butt. I wanted bigger breast. At my old school all the boys would talk about my big butt. Girls were always jealous of my long hair. That's the only great thing Brenda gave me. I get my pretty chinky eyes from my daddy. He's so handsome. I look like a girl version of him. While Keke was in the bathroom Tiffany finished what she started. Tiffany proceeds to rubbing her clitoris with her fingers while thinking of Dawson.

Little John

Laying low was the best thing I could be doing right now. I popped Tyron a few weeks ago for Skip. He never saw it coming. I walked up on him as he was headed to the Chinese store. It was as around one in the morning I wore all black with my hoodie low. Tyron is taller than me so I stayed walking behind him undetected . As soon as he got to the step of the store, pop right to the back of his head. I didn't watch him but I knew he was dead. I saw his brains come out. After I did the deed I ran and threw the gun in the sewer. I threw up in the bushes later. My first kill and I plan doing it again. I'm gonna take over Philly. Once I get all I need from Skip. I miss my sisters though. I have to figure out how to see Tiffany and Vanessa.

James didn't know what he was missing with making money. John and James parted ways after John decided he was stepping up from being a carrier. James wasn't built like that, he has a loving mother. Little John laid back on his futon and started smoking his blunt. He takes his bank roll out his pocket.

Skips baby mom comes in the room. "Yo Jay food is done. Are you eating?" "Yeah I'll be down."

Skip made his way to become Jax's right hand man. Jax is the "Man" of Southwest. He's damn near impossible to touch. It was Skips dream to be promoted. Skip thinks small time to John. John sat at the table with Skip and his children. Skip has three darling daughters Monica, Shana and Luz. Luz is the same age as John. Monica is the oldest. John has never met Monica. Skip sent her away for school. Her behavior is something he said he's never seen in a girl. Skip describes Monica as if she was supposed to be a boy instead. John enjoys staying at Skips house. It's big, clean, and everything he wants in a home. Everyone has their own bed and he is eating a home cooked meal. No Ramen noodles or hotdogs and baked beans. John hates baked beans, especially how Brenda or Grandma Mabel cooked them. All that syrup and sugar on beans! Eww! John is so happy not to be living like that anymore.

"John you are the man. You are my man boy! Your birthday is coming up right?"

"Yeah."

"We're gonna celebrate it all!"

After dinner John went upstairs to change clothes for tonight's work. Luz was waiting for him in the room. She closed the door quickly. John hurried up and pulled down his sweatpants. Luz pulled down her jeans and bent over on the bed. The two teenagers quickly had sex. Skip was outside in the car conducting business to his soldiers. Skip's baby mother and Shana were downstairs in the dining room. No one suspected the two had been seeing each other. Luz came on to John his first night in the house. Luz is known in middle school for going in the bathrooms with boys and girls. She lost her virginity officially to John. She was attracted to his hard ways. Never smiling and always so serious. On John's first night in their luxurious house on Cobbs Creek Parkway, Luz snuck into his room and laid next to him. John was startled and at first uncomfortable when Luz got in the bed. She kissed his cheek and put her hand down his pants. What does this pretty girl want with me? She keeps her distance from him while everyone is at home together. As far as he could tell she wouldn't be interested in him. But here Luz was sneaking in his room every night before he went out to do street work.

John got in the car with Skip and Hazel. Skip hands John a fresh burner for his next target. "My nigga down South Philly need some work done. A bull name Lay. If we can do this, we will expand ya heard." John nods. Hazel is John's back up for the night. Lay is known to be crewed up. Hazel is a more experienced hitter. She's been working for Skip now for six months. Prior she was in the badlands but her crew got locked or murdered. Hazel and John put on face masks since it's about twenty degrees outside and they won't come off alarming. They get out of Skips black bonneville and walk the rest of the way. Skip stays behind so after the deed he can swoop around and get them. There were three black dudes sitting on the corner of Reed Street. They were using crates as chairs. Hazel signaled John that Lay was present amongst the crew.

Underneath the hoodie and ski mask is a bad bitch. Hazel was five foot five, light skin, long thick black hair. She had a peach shaped booty and nice size breast. Hazel had been working for Lay for two weeks. She knew where he stayed and his wife. After the signal John and Hazel unloaded their guns on all the dudes sitting down. In the corner was another boy who came out of nowhere he started running. John shot him without hesitation. Skip came back with the car just in time. Just like that the deed was done.

Mabel

It feels so good to be home. Since Mabel came back to the south she has never felt more alive. The only thing Mabel wished was that Brenda came down with her to clean herself up and raise the children out here. She has been staying in her childhood home that's owned by Sunny. Mabel went inside of her parents old room and started looking at their childhood pictures that stood upon the cherry wood dresser. She began reminiscing when she saw the picture of her and Todd Senior. All of Mabel's family lives between Virginia and North Carolina. She and her eldest sister Hattie were the only two to venture up north. Hattie lived in New York City with her husband before she died. Hattie went to New York looking to make it big in singing. She did accomplish one album before settling down and having children. Now it's just Mabel and

Sunny. Sunny has made an excellent life in North Carolina. He's a landlord to many properties and owns a farm.

Mabel is the only one who didn't prosper from living in Philadelphia. Mabel met her husband Todd while working at a bank as a teller. He promised her the world. Mabel was a late bloomer so she didn't know she was being manipulated and later on abused.

Todd senior wined and dined Mabel. They got married after six months and she got pregnant with Todd immediately. Todd purchased a beautiful home in the Overbrook section of West Philadelphia. Everything was a dream to Mabel. They would host parties and dinners for local artists. Todd played the bass and piano. There were times when he would be on the road for a couple months at a time. Mabel didn't mind that she was busy raising Todd and working at the bank. One day Todd came home from a show in New York with a new darkness within him. He started beating Todd and cursing out Mabel for the oddest of things. Todd would spend the majority of his time in his room hidden. He didn't want to get in his father's way. That didn't stop Todd from going into his son's room with his belt to beat him for something he assumed he did. "What's going on Todd? What have I done to make you treat me this way?" Is all Mabel would say. Todd wouldn't respond instead he would take off his belt and beat Mabel and Todd like children. Mabel would go to work in ninety degree weather with long sleeves on just so no one would see the bruises. Todd's band had broken up and Mabel had to maintain all household responsibilities. If dinner wasn't cooked and the house clean Todd would start his rage.

Mabel one day was doing laundry and almost stuck herself with a needle that was in Todd's pants. That's when she discovered her husband was a junkie. But where is he shooting up on his body? I see no marks on his arms. Mabel begged Todd to get help. Todd had got clean of drugs for a little while. That's how Brenda was conceived. Mabel swore her family was back on track. Todd had started working at a neighborhood hardware store. But there was something different about Little Todd.

Todd had started getting into fights at school. He was accused of inappropriately touching female classmates. She almost lost her job at the bank due to the school constantly calling for her to pick up Todd. Her husband stopped coming home. Mabel felt like she was losing it. Her son turned into this terror she couldn't control. She had no one to help her out. There were times when Brenda would just cry and cry as if she felt Mabel's pain. Mabel started giving her cough syrup so she would go to sleep and Mabel would have peace of mind.

The last time Mabel saw Todd Lawrence Jackson Senior was at the morgue to identify his body. By then she had met Patricia's father and he got her back on track. She worked for him at night as a high class whore and worked the bank like usual. She gave Todd and Brenda's father a proper burial. He was still her husband. At her late husband's funeral she found out he had another son named Lawrence that lived in New Jersey with his grandmother because his mother overdosed. Todd Senior has two ex wives and has been battling drugs for the majority of his life. He would shoot up in between his toes. Which explained why he always wore socks.

Being a high class prostitute was short lived. Mabel got pregnant with Patricia and found out her new love Nathan was happily married to a woman named Carol. Carol couldn't have children. Mabel started drinking to ease the heartache. Nathan caught Mabel one night so drunk off moonshine passed out on the kitchen floor. Todd had Patricia with her diaper open claiming her was about to change her but Nathan didn't see any diaper changing items. He grabbed Patricia and left. Carol accepted Patricia and dealt with the heartache of her husband cheating on her. They took Patricia to the doctor the next day to make sure she wasn't being abused. Thankfully there was no sign of abuse. Nathan could only imagine if he hadn't come by what would have been. Mabel was so deep in her alcoholism she neglected Todd and Brenda. She had to whore the old fashioned way walking the streets at night and going to ghetto bars to pick up 'Johns'. She brought the men home sometimes. Nathan took Mabel to court for Patricia and allowed her to have visitation rights. When Mabel would sober up and when Patricia was old enough to take care of herself he would let her spend the day with Mabel. Brenda was always jealous of Patricia.

Mabel was so lost in her memories of the past she almost missed Brenda's call.

"Yes child."

"Mom you need to come off vacation! Little John still ain't home! Someone bust one of my windows with a brick!"

"Brenda I don't think I'm coming back! Now I have told you to call the police! Who are you upset with now? Huh!"

"You know I can't call the police!"

"Go up to the school dummy! Lord, I know I should've done better by you! I'm hanging up"

"Mom-" Mabel hung up on Brenda. I can't keep on with that girl. She's gonna learn.

Brenda

How could my mother do this to me? Leave me all alone!!!

Brenda knows who threw that brick. It was Divine's daughter

Chante. That little bitch gotta be like fifteen now. I should

send for one of Aunt Hattie's granddaughters from New York.

Yeah I think that's how I'm gonna play it. Divine wanna play

we gonna play! I ain't going up to Little John school you

know what fuck him too. Robert has been ducking me since I

told him Little John maybe his. Fuck all of them! I got my

Nessa. Vanessa sat on the edge of Brenda's bed playing with

her Barbie Doll. Brenda took a swig of her colt forty five and

called Joy at the check cashing place next. I ain't heard from

her since the funeral.

"Joy what the hell is up?"

"I'm working Brenda. How are you?"

"Bitch Divine wants war! Her daughter threw a brick in my house! Busted up my window! My Mama done left me to go live down south with my Uncle! Shit is fucked up around here! I need you!"

Joy looks at the phone and is not an ounce shocked at anything that is happening to Brenda.

"What do you need me to do Brenda? I talked to Pat. I know Little John is gone! I'm telling you up front about this but I'm going to see John soon. I was gonna call you and tell you later."

Brenda is in a pit of rage just hearing John's name besides her own son feels her up with hate. "Fuck you!!!! You betray me?!? I got you dirty ass bitch! You think you better than me cause yo man make you go to church?!? That's why you can't have kids dirty bitch!!!"

"I can't have kids courtesy of Todd!!! He raped me, did you forget? You know what I hope you get all you deserve coming to your crackhead ass and you best pray we never cross paths again!" Joy hung up the phone.

Brenda gets up from her bed and starts screaming to the top of her lungs.

"FUCKIN' LIARS!!!" Vanessa starts crying out of confusion. Brenda looks at her and calms her down. "Mommy sorry Nessy...stop crying. People are trying to hurt me and you!" Vanessa stops crying and asks. " Who is trying to hurt us?"

"Don't worry Mommy gonna handle it all." Brenda made one more phone call.

Patricia

Pat stood in the school yard waiting for Little John to come out. When he saw her from a distance he was shocked. Pat noticed that Little John had on new clothes and sneakers. He picked up weight and grew a few inches taller he had to be at least five foot eight.

"Little John! I mean just John huh you ain't so little ha!" John gave his Aunt the biggest loving hug ever. "I'm not going home Auntie if that's why you're here." Pat stares at John. She wanted to ask him so many questions but she didn't want to scare him away. "I just came to make sure you're safe. I came around the school awhile back but you were not here. I just want you to know that you can always come home with us." John put his head down for a moment. "Thanks Auntie but I'm my own man now. I got to go. Give this to Tiffany for me."

Patricia takes the envelope and it feels like money maybe in it. Oh my God! What is this boy into! "John, do you wanna come with us to see your dad Saturday?"

John didn't respond, he just kept walking. Patricia knew what that meant. That boy is gone. I'm glad he still attends school for now.

Later on that night...

"Tiffany can you come here!" Patricia yelled from the bottom of the stairs.

Tiffany came down the stairs curious to what her Aunt wanted. Pat handed Tiffany the envelope Little John gave her. "What's this?"

"I don't know, it's from your brother. I went to his school today."

Tiffany opened the envelope and saw a note and a bunch of twenty dollar bills. Patricia looked at the money. Tiffany read the note and started to cry. Patricia took the note and read it. *'Sis I love you and I'm fine. Here's some money and when I can I will send more. Don't look for me.'*

Patricia hugged Tiffany. She felt helpless. This boy is out here in the streets! I have to tell John. "Tiffany we will talk to your dad about this Saturday. Ok?" Patricia took the envelope and sat down on the couch. She began counting the money. It was a total of two hundred sixty dollars. Tiffany sat down next to her Aunt. "What are you gonna do with the money?" Pat shook her head. Then shrugged her shoulders. What am I going to do with this money? She counted out one hundred dollars and put it aside. "I'm gonna put money up for your father. We can use the rest to take you to get new clothes and braids. I'm tired of that ponytail. Your hair has even started to fall out or are pulling your hair again? Do you want to go back to child guidance?" Tiffany put her head down and decided she better shape up because she didn't want to go back to the hospital. "No Aunt Pat, I'm gonna do right. We can get my hair done. I won't pull it out no more." Tiffany went upstairs. Pat started preparing for another day when the phone rings. At first she didn't want to answer. She didn't recognize the number.

"Hello."

"Pat it's Joy. I'm so sorry to bother you. Are you free one afternoon this week? Before the children get home? I really need to talk to you."

"Yeah sure Joy. You can come by around one." She hangs up the phone. Oh shit I know this involves Brenda somehow. The phone rings again but it's Jake this time. "Hey baby!" Jake greets his loving wife.

"Hey. How are you?" Patricia asks as twirls the phone cord debating on telling Jake about Little John. Jake explains to Pat that they are on high alert at work because the temperatures are dropping below freezing. We just got over the biggest blizzard in the beginning of the year. I haven't seen my husband all week. "Honey I'm gonna take Tiffany to see John Saturday. I think Little John is in the streets. Joy wants to meet one day this week...I'm sure it's about Brenda. I'm trying to hold it together!"

"Baby if Little John is in the street there ain't much you can do. Why do you say that anyway? Did something happen?"

"He's been missing and I went up to the school he gave me an envelope to give to Tiffany. It had two hundred sixty dollars inside. A note too!"

"Brenda put him out, what do you expect Pat?"

"I don't know for him to come to us?"

"Pat if he out in the streets that means he was already in them before she kicked him out. Don't be so naïve! Now how are the kids inside our home? My boys and Keke?"

"Everyone is good Jake. JJ won a dance contest!" Pat and Jake always made sure their conversations ended in a positive manner. They hang up and the phone rings yet again. It's a damn hotline tonight!

"Yes?" Pat is somewhat annoyed.

"Can I speak with Tiffany please it's Mark."

Pat yells again for Tiffany to come downstairs.

"Yes Aunt Pat?"

"Phone for you, it's Mark. Make it short, it's getting late!"

Tiffany

Tiffany had not spoken to Mark in months and then he just called out of the blue. Telling this story that he was shot in the shoulder coming around the corner awhile back and how he told his Uncle Jacob to call her. He asked her to come visit him after school. She wanted to but a part of her didn't. Mark could be lying I mean for sympathy. I don't even know why he was ever put in the hospital either. Tiffany debates about it all day in school. Tiffany's little school boyfriend Rico noticed her distance. Rico was something to do so she didn't feel stupid if Dawson was playing her how Mark did.

"Tiff baby, who do you not love me today?" Rico is from Puerto Rico and is still learning how to speak English. Tiffany looked him up and down. He was so easy to manipulate. He gave Tiffany his lunch money everyday. That plus he was fine. He doesn't know Tiffany's story. Like some of the other students who whisper about her walking down the halls. All the rumors about her seducing her Uncle and Father made Tiffany crazy at times. Once a week she met with the guidance counselor at school. Tiffany had been in four fights this school year. The most she has ever been in. Tiffany was not being labeled a victim to anybody.

"I'm loving you baby!" She hugs Rico and kisses him on the cheek. I'll go see what the hell Mark is talking about, Tiffany decided.

Mark couldn't wait to see Tiffany. He could see her walking up the block while sitting on his steps. Tiffany could see Mark and she noticed Mark had flowers in his hand. Once she came up towards Mark he reached out and hugged Tiffany so tight. "I'm sorry Tiffany. I miss you so much!" Tiffany was shocked to hear those words come out of Mark's mouth.

"I missed you too. So tell me what happened to you." They went in the house and sat on the couch they once cuddled to sleep in. Mark gave Tiffany her flowers. She never received flowers before. "Yo I got shot on Reed Street! They started shooting when I was coming up and then I tried to run but I got hit in the shoulder! Next thing I know I'm in the hospital!" Mark showed Tiffany his bullet wound. I can't believe he was really shot. "I would've come to see you. If I knew... I thought you didn't like me anymore." Mark kissed Tiffany on the lips. Oh no he's making me like him all over again. "Mark why were you in the hospital with me?" Mark laid Tiffany on his chest.

"They say I'm bipolar cause I get in trouble sometimes. I got out of going to juvie because of my Uncle. I stole a car." Tiffany laid there and wondered what is bipolar? But she didn't want to ask him. He's probably going to think I'm stupid.

"Oh ok that's not so bad."

"Really? They give me meds for it but sometimes I don't take them. My Uncle said we were moving far away but I don't want to!" Mark started kissing Tiffany and pulling her shirt off. Moments later the two are naked on the couch and Tiffany is on top of Mark riding him hard. I can't believe I'm doing it to Mark...this feels so good. I don't want to stop. "Mark can we be together?" Tiffany asks as she strokes Mark. Mark was in a sexual drunk trance from Tiffany. He really liked Tiffany and the sex he was receiving. "Yeah...I'll be your boyfriend." The words made Tiffany so happy and right before the two lovers climax Mark's uncle Jacob came into the house. He saw two naked teenagers sweating up his fancy couch. "Mark why wouldn't you at least go upstairs?" Tiffany grabbed her clothes off the floor and tried to cover herself as much as possible. Mark put his head down as he hurriedly put on his jeans. "I'm sorry Unc.."

Jacob turned around so Tiffany could get dressed. Tiffany looked at the clock on the wall. Oh shit it's 7:30 p.m. I was supposed to be home by 7:00 p.m. "Mr. Jacob, I'm sorry. I really am, I have to leave, I'm past my curfew." Jacob could see the concern in Tiffany's eyes and after Mark was shot he wouldn't dare allow her to go home on the bus. "Come on Tiffany we will take you home."

Pat was downstairs waiting for Tiffany. "Aunt Pat I was at Mark's house and his Uncle gave me a ride home. See that's them outside in the Lexus. They wanna meet you." Pat wanted to be mad at Tiffany but since she was safe and was with an adult she went outside and introduced herself. Patricia saw the Lexus and immediately asked Jake "Are you a drug dealer?" Jake and Mark burst out into laughter. Pat face remained serious. " Honey no I'm a lawyer. Here's my card." He handed Pat his business card: It read Jake Lewis Esquire Attorney at Law. Pat placed her hand on her chest with relief. "I'm

Patricia, Tiffany's Aunt. Nice to meet y'all can y'all have her home on time please?"

"Of course we are moving in a couple weeks so Mark is gonna have to come spend time down here sometime or I come get her and drop her off myself."

"Where are you moving to?"

"The Northeast by Franklin Mills. Mark was shot. He's like a son more than a nephew. I gotta protect him."

"My goodness I see. Well we will work something out. Y'all have a good night." Tiffany and Pat went inside. Tiffany ran upstairs to the bathroom immediately. She jumped right in the shower thinking about how good it was to be with Mark. He said yes to being my boyfriend!! I'm so happy he's so fine but why does he have to live so far away?

Pat

I need to talk to these girls about sex I feel they are having it. In fact I know they are. I saw a hickey on Keke's neck! The last thing I need is to be a young grandmother! I know I had her young but she doesn't have to be like me. Pat sat patiently in the living room waiting for Joy to come over. She had two shots of vodka to calm her nerves because she knew Brenda was definitely involved. Pat heard the doorbell ring and immediately got up. It was Joy. She let her in. "Hey Joy it's good to see you. What's going on?" Joy took off her coat and immediately sat down. "I know you figured it's about Brenda. I wanted to come over sooner but I have been busy. I plan on visiting John real soon. I told that to Brenda and she went off! I told her I know Little John ran away too. I know cause I've seen him...but I ain't tell Brenda that part."

Pat eyes widened "Seen him where?"

"He is on a corner around Willows Avenue. I didn't approach him though he wasn't with regular type boys. He was with grown ass men selling." Pat knew it!

"Fuck! That's it Joy?"

"No…so after I told Brenda I was going to visit John she was like that's why you can't have kids and I told her Pat I told her…" Pat grabs Joy by the shoulders. "You told her what?!?" Joy starts to cry. Oh fuck Pat gets up from the couch and gets her hidden blunt she keeps in a locked draw in the dining room. Pat lights it up and takes a long drag. The fuck she is about to tell me? Pat passes the blunt to Joy; she quickly puffs it in between cries. Joy gathers a high strength to finish telling Pat the truth.

"Todd raped me when we were kids. I spent the night and Brenda thought it would be funny to lock me in Todd's room." Patricia's heart dropped to her stomach. She suddenly felt sick and ready to vomit. "She put something up against the door. I think Todd was sleeping. He heard me yell at Brenda and woke up. He asked if I was coming to give him a surprise. He said Brenda told him I liked him. I told him I wanted to leave out but he already locked the door from the inside. He grabbed me.." Tears flowed endlessly down Joy's face and Patricia became filled with rage. Why would Brenda do such a thing! She's the Goddamn Devil, her and Mabel both!

"Where was Mabel?" Pat had to ask.

"She wasn't home, Pat. He took my virginity and I tried to tell Brenda...she said I was lying!" Joy hits the blunt again. Pat gets up again to grab that bottle of vodka. Patricia opened the bottle and gave it to Joy. Joy takes a few hits and then puts the bottle on the floor.

"Did you scream for help?" Joy shook her head no.

"He choked me unconscious. Brenda said I was lying and that I just had sex with Todd...now I'm claiming he raped me cause I could get in trouble. For the rest of the summer I didn't go over there. I stayed at my grandma's house in Delaware. When school started back up I didn't have a choice but to be Brenda's friend she said she would tell the whole school and my Mom! I was only eleven and Todd had to be eighteen. Then when he raped that young girl you remember Tanya?"

"I can never forget..."

"Brenda said everyone was lying. I fuckin' hate her Pat! I can't have children! Then I had to sit back and watch her drag that good man down! I tried to break them up. I called Divine when she was messing with her boyfriend! She just kept winning Pat!" Patricia looked at Joy and couldn't believe how horrible this whole thing had turned out to be. My family are monsters! I'm glad Todd is dead and I'm glad Mabel left. Patricia got up from the couch and started pacing. Poor John. The children Tiffany, Little John, and Vanessa! Vanessa she's still with Brenda Oh God! What can I do? Joy sat there staring at Patricia wondering what's going through her mind. "Pat, are you okay? I'm sorry to tell you all this but shit has hit the fan! She said something about war with Divine too!"

"War? What is she talking about? Because she got beat up?"

"Not just that...Divine's daughter busted the window out."

"Aw shit we got to get Vanessa out of there...Hmmm I'm gonna make nice with Mabel and get information out of her. I think I have a plan."

Visiting Daddy

Tiffany couldn't wait to see her Dad, Saturday couldn't come fast enough. She got her hair braided the night before. Tiffany's head felt a little sore but she didn't care. Today she could actually hug her father. As soon as John was in eye contact Tiffany ran and jumped in her Father's arms. "Daddy I miss you! I love you!" Tiffany kissed John's face over and over again. John hugged Tiffany tight. "I miss you too and you know I love you!" Patricia watched them reunite with tears in her eyes. John and Patricia hugged. Everyone sat at the table holding hands and smiling. "Dad have you gotten my letters?"

"No I haven't. Did you get mine?"

Tiffany shook her head no.

"Is the mail running slow in here?" Patricia asks John.

"I don't know Pat. I see everyone else get their mail. Thank you for the money on my books! I hope I'm not burdening you and Jake." Patricia rolled her eyes in her head.

"I don't want to ruin this happy day but know that things have really changed, John and not for the better for some of us."

"I can only imagine I know Little John is not home with Brenda. Jake told me. I really appreciate him taking my calls at work. He's good with a C.O. I wonder if he could help me find out what's going on with the letters." John scratches his head and stares at Tiffany. Tiffany sits there wondering what her Father is thinking. Does he think I'm a bad daughter? Does he feel bad for saving me? John turns his head to Patricia with concern. "If you see Little John again tell him I want to see him." Patricia nods her yes. "Tiffany, be careful out here with these boys. You're growing up and I know how it is. These boys ain't no good Tiff. None of them." Tiffany nods her head. "Daddy I'm getting ready to go to high school.

I made an honor roll this quarter!" Tiffany pulls her report card out of her pocket. John is pleased to see straight A's. "I'm not gonna pull my hair out anymore either. I wrote it in a letter...I'm gonna do better. I promise."

"I know you will baby." They both smile at each other making their chinky eyes shrink into their cheeks. Tiffany is a split image of John. "Pat is there anyway you can get Vanessa?" Patricia was hesitant to answer but she had to say it even with Tiffany present. "Mabel left to live down south. She gave me the last known number she had for Derrick but it doesn't work. We gotta get Vanessa out of that house. Brenda is back at it. Her and Joy got into it. There is so much I need to tell you but I don't wanna upset Tiffany." Tiffany sat at the table looking puzzled. Is she talking about cousin Derrick? But why call him? Tiffany felt compelled to ask so she did. I don't want to be in the dark anything anymore. "Why did you call cousin Derrick, Aunt Pat?" John and Pat looked at each other and agreed. " Your sister Vanessa is his child not mine. I had not touched your mother in months and then boom she's pregnant. I got word that Brenda had been cheating on me with him." Tiffany's face balled up with disgust. That nasty bitch Brenda. "What? That's nasty why you didn't leave her? And take us with you?"

"I love all of you and I just fell apart Tiffany. I let myself go…I tried to leave your mother and every time I made a way she would do something to destroy my plans. It's my own fault. After you were born for a while she was good, at least she was good to me. I guess I really didn't know Brenda. I didn't want to believe how messed up she was…everyone warned me."

Tiffany learned a lot about her Dad that visit. He told her about his basketball highlights in college. John told Tiffany about his other sister Nora who lives in Africa as a teacher. Tiffany only knew about her aunt Divine whom she had not seen in years. Patricia promised Tiffany she would put her in touch with her father's side of the family again. John and Tiffany took pictures. Tiffany didn't tell her Dad about Mark. She figured she would wait to tell him in a letter. Tiffany walked out from her father's jail visit feeling better about the situation at hand.

On the ride back home Tiffany couldn't wait to ask her Aunt a ton of questions.

"Aunt Pat, I didn't want to ask Daddy cause I don't want to upset him but I gotta know…"

"Know what Tiffany?"

"Is Little John my dad son? He doesn't look like any of us. I mean me and Nessa look alike sort of." Pat let's out a long sigh before telling Tiffany the truth.

"Tiffany you are John's only child. We don't know who Little John Dad is..I'm sure Brenda does, maybe. I mean who knows. You know I didn't exactly grow up with her and Todd." Tiffany remembered hearing Brenda say nasty things about Pat being raised by her pimp father. Brenda would tell whoever dared to listen that Patricia is a bastard and that her father kidnapped her. "Yeah Brenda said nasty things about you and your family."

"My father was a pimp... he told me before he died the truth. I'm glad to have had him in my life. Who knows maybe Todd would've raped me too...sorry Tiffany..."

"I know what you mean Aunt Pat."

"I do want to talk to you and Keke about something tomorrow. We will have a nice breakfast and be open with each other."

What would she want to talk to me and Keke about? We've been doing our chores. I have been coming home on time.

Keke don't come home sometimes since she started having real sex.

Breakfast with Aunt Patricia

Tiffany could smell the food in her dreams. Aunt Pat is really doing it up. When Tiffany got home last night she kind of warned Keke that her mother wanted to talk to them during breakfast. Keke was nervous about having breakfast with her mother. That morning Keke tried to play sick. "Tiff tell my mom I don't feel good. I got bad cramps." Tiffany pulls the covers off Keke. "Girl stop playing. I don't think we are in trouble! She didn't sound mad to me." Keke rolls over. "She never sounds mad. She does get mad sometimes...you just ain't seen it yet. She is probably making us breakfast as a trap." Tiffany sucked her teeth at Keke and started pulling at her braids. I don't want to go downstairs if it's a trap. But what did we do?

"Girls come downstairs, the food is now ready." Pat yelled from the bottom of the stairs.

"We are coming , Aunt Pat!" Tiffany grabs Keke and forces her off the bed. Keke falls down to the floor. " What y'all doing up there?" Patricia yells again.

"Keke playing around! Here we come!" Tiffany assures Pat. Keke and Tiffany creep down the stairs slowly. Patricia is sitting at the dining room table. She made the twins eat cereal earlier. The boys played with their puzzles on the living room floor. Keke and Tiffany sat down to pancakes, cheese grits, cheese eggs, and turkey sausage. They immediately dug in. Tiffany noticed that Patricia wasn't really eating her breakfast. "What's wrong Aunt Pat?"

"Girls…I noticed a change in you two this year. I want to go about this the right way…so I'm just gonna ask it even though I know the answer, so please don't lie to me." Both girls looked at Patricia with concern. "Are you two having sex? I don't want to be nobody's thirty year old grandma!" Tiffany put her fork down and started thinking the worst. If I say yes what if she kicks me out! Oh no tell my Dad even!

Keke immediately lies. "No Mommy I do kiss my boyfriend sometimes but sex is nasty." Patricia rolled her eyes at Keke. She really thinks I'm stupid. "Tiffany?"

"Uh I did it once. Are you gonna kick me out?" Patricia looked at Tiffany. "No I'm not kicking you out. However you are both going to the doctors." Keke started crying. "Why do I gotta go to the doctors Mommy? I'm not doing nothing!"

"Keona don't make me angry! Alright? Now I'm not stupid! I saw marks on your neck! Don't make my mistakes." Keke looks at her Mother and tears just flow down her face. "You gonna tell Daddy on me?" Patricia doesn't answer Keke right away. Instead she starts to eat her breakfast and sip her coffee. Keke is in an uproar. "Mom don't tell Daddy!! I won't do it anymore, I promise!"

Tiffany sits at the table watching her fifteen year old cousin act a fool. She tries so hard not to burst out laughing in her face. "I won't say anything Keke but I'm sure he can tell. Men can smell hot pussy, virgin pussy, and fast pussy. Ya understand me?"

Tiffany never heard her Aunt speak like that before. We must have made her mad.

After breakfast Tiffany decided to tell her Aunt about stealing Brenda's birth control.

"I was scared Aunt Pat..." Patricia really didn't know what she was signing up for when raising a rape victim, even if it is her own niece.

Tiffany

Being with Mark is so much fun. It takes a long time to get to his house if Aunt Pat doesn't drive me but I don't care. Sometimes his Uncle is home and most of the time he isn't. I get to be with my boyfriend all day. We get to have sex all day long and go to McDonalds. Since his Uncle is barely home sometimes we go in the kitchen and do it on the countertop. He drives me so wild. Since he's a little older Mark is more experienced. He knows how to make me scream. Dawson was good but not like Mark. Today he's coming to my house though. Which is going to be boring, but Aunt Pat said so. He can't be in my room like at his house. We are going to have to go off somewhere to have privacy. He said he would be here by noon. I have plenty of time to get ready. Keke sat on the bed watching Tiffany get dressed. "At least you get to still see Mark without sneaking...I hate my dad!" Tiffany watched

Keke pout and began to cry. Keke was put on punishment and wasn't allowed to see Kevin anymore. Jake came home early and caught Keke walking up to the house with Kevin. Kevin saw Jake and ran. Keke was so scared she just started crying because she thought if she did she wouldn't get in trouble. That was the first time Jake ever hit Keke. Aunt Pat took Keke to the family doctor to get checked out the next day. Pat already knew Keke was lying about having sex. Jake's cousin works at the doctor's office and called Pat later that day to tell her about Keke's appointment.

"You shouldn't have lied Keke. I told you to stop sneaking out. You already see him at school and after school."

"Shut up Tiffany. It took me a week to get him back. He's terrified of my Dad!"

"Who wouldn't be? Hahahaha!" Tiffany continues to get dressed. Keke throws a pillow at Tiffany and mouths 'shut up'.

It was 12:30 p.m. and Mark still hadn't gotten to Tiffany's house. It was a nice day so Tiffany decided to sit outside and wait for him. While she was waiting she saw a familiar face walking up towards the house. It can't be! " Oh my God, Janell!" Tiffany ran up and hugged her. Tiffany has not seen Janell since the seventh grade. "Hey Tiffany I just came back home from New Jersey. School lets out early there. I'm going to high school here in Philly. I beg my dad! He left my mom girl…"

"Wow for real? I was wondering if I would see you again. I miss you so much!"

"I miss you too B.F.F. I wasn't allowed to talk to anybody from Philly. My Pops was being mad strict! But me and his new boo don't get along. I give her hell she ain't my Mom!" Both girls started laughing. The two noticed a red car pulling up to park. It looked like a Benz. "Who is that?" Janell asked. Mark gets out of the car. Oh no whose car is that Tiffany's wondering. Mark comes over and hugs Tiffany. "Mark where did you get that car?" Mark smiles. "We are going out, baby. Whose this?"

"This is my best friend Janell. Where are we going? I didn't know you could drive."

"Hell yeah I can drive. Come on y'all." The girls get in the car.

Tiffany was enjoying riding around the hood in a Benz. Tiffany thought of Little John and how he would be with Mark. I miss my brother. Tiffany felt herself about to shift into her thoughts but she got out of it. She looked at Mark and was so happy to be with him. He's so cute. "Mark can we go around Willows Ave? I want to see if Little John is around there."

"Yup." They drove straight down Willows Avenue for four blocks. No sign of Little John. Tiffany kept her composure. I know I will see my brother again. Mark drove the girls to the basketball ball court in South Philly. "I miss it here Tiff. I just want to play a few games then we can take ya friend home." Tiffany rolled her eyes and then agreed. It will give me and Janell time to catch up. Mark parked the car, gave Tiffany a quick kiss, and ran out to the basketball court. Tiffany and Janell got out of the car. They decided to find a Chinese store.

"What was it like living in New Jersey?"

"Boring as hell! I wanted to be there for you Tiffany. I just wanted you to know but my Pops saw my Mom on porn and went crazy."

"Ya Mom does porn?"

"Apparently for some time too. I'm staying at my grandma's house now. My Mom is cool though. She got a rich boyfriend."

"Hmmm...why can't you live with her?"

"I will soon after the custody thing gets settled. Shit I rather be with her and be rich. Then stay with my broke ass Pops and his Mom."

"Where does she live?"

"In Overbrook. In this big ass house. I took the bus to see her."

The girls walked back to the court to see Mark being the star of the court as usual. His gunshot wound doesn't stop his show. Tiffany noticed a couple of girls eyeing Mark from the sidelines. Oh here we go. Tiffany gets Janell attention and points to the girls. "What are you gonna do if they step to Mark?"

"See what Mark does and then go from there."

Tiffany and Janell watched Mark and cheered for him. The girls that were eyeing Mark had left after the third game.

Mark played one more game and then parted ways from his friends. "Did you see me Tiff?"

"Yes I saw you. What are gonna do now?"

"Go to McDonalds drive thru and then take ya friend home."

Mark treated both girls to McDonalds and then dropped Janell off at her grandma's house. "Let's go to the park." Mark says to Tiffany as he rubs her thigh. Mark drives them to Parkside by the Mann Center. Tiffany couldn't wait to get in the back seat of the Benz. She immediately took her shorts off and instructed Mark to kiss her vagina. Oh I love that feeling. Tiffany throws Mark head deeper inside her vagina. Mark gets up from pleasuring Tiffany and pulls his basketball shorts down. Tiffany opens her mouth wide and starts sucking Mark off. The two lovers get really wild in the backseat of the Benz. So wild and loud that there's a tap at the window. Tiffany wipes the steam off the window to see two white police officers. Tiffany and Mark are settled. "I need you two dressed and roll down all the windows!" The officer instructed. They both did as they were told. "This car was reported stolen. You're both under arrest! Come out with your hands up!" Mark gives Tiffany a big kiss and hugs her. "I'm sorry. I just wanted us to have fun today." Tiffany and Mark are arrested.

Pat

What have I gotten myself into? I really wonder if I am doing the right thing sometimes with these girls? Keke is getting out of control! She didn't come home last night. Jake has a cop friend on the job looking for her. Tiffany has her ways but at least she comes home. I'm glad that boy took the whole rap from that stolen car but I have noticed a change in her since he's been gone. She seems depressed again and pulls out her hair. Damn it what am I gonna do for this girl birthday? Keke had fun at Dave and Busters for hers. I doubt Tiffany would want to do the same thing. JJ comes rushing in the room during Pat's rants to herself. "Yo Mommy! Can we go to the park?" Pat starts to laugh. "Boy who are you saying yo to? Where did you get that from?"

"We say it at camp! So can we go?"

"Yes later ok. Mommy is thinking. Where's Tiffany?"

"She's outside with Nelly."

" Ha oh you mean Janell?"

"I call her Nelly. She said when I grow up we can get married." JJ smiles as he makes this statement.

"Go on downstairs boy!"

That boy is a mess. Patricia gets on the phone to make a call she should have made but she had been dragging her feet to do so. I hope this cheers her up.

"Hello."

"Hi can I speak to Ms. Lily please?"

"This is her. Who is this?"

"Hi…um this is Patricia. Your granddaughter Tiffany's aunt."

"Oh you ain't calling me on no bull shit are you? Your sister is gonna catch a beat down real soon!! Keep calling here talking shit! Divine gonna see her , you watch!"

"Ma'am no! Listen I'm calling for Tiffany. John wants you to see her. I figure since her birthday is next week it would be a nice surprise for her."

There was a long pulse on the phone.

"Okay. I don't want no shit ya understand."

"Yes, I understand. I will call you next week. Thank you Ms. Lily." Patricia hangs up the phone and sits on her bed. What kind of shit is Brenda getting into? I thought Ms. Lily was a kind and sweet old lady but I guess Brenda has brought out the worst in her. The phone rings, Patricia almost didn't want to pick up. I don't want any more bad or outrageous news!

"Hello."

"Yeah this is Officer Gordon. I have your daughter Keke. We picked her up in South Philadelphia. She was at a local bus stop. I'm about to bring her home."

"Thank you so much."

Great...I'm sure Jake already heard about it. I will wait for him to call me.

About twenty five minutes later Keke walks through the door. Officer Gordon greets Patricia and leaves. Tiffany, the twins and Janell are having lunch in the dining room.

Patricia slaps Keke in the face. "What the fuck is wrong with you?" Keke cries and runs up the stairs. Patricia follows Keke upstairs. Moments later all you hear are Keke's screams. The twins start giggling to themselves. "Keke getting a beat in'!" Tiffany and Janell continue to eat their hoagies and not say a word.

Tiffany's Visit to Grandma Lily

I'm so nervous. I'm seeing my grandma today on my dad's side! I don't remember much at all. I just know that they hated Brenda with a passion. Through that hate came separation, like my Dad was kicked out of their family. It's the day before my birthday. I hope she gives me money or something. If she don't like me then fuck her. I miss Mark so much. I can't believe he's locked up this time. Usually his Uncle can get him out of this type of stuff, but I guess not this time.

On my way to Lily's house Pat was doing her best to coach Tiffany for this visit.

"Now ya know Brenda got some shit going be prepared for her that."

"When don't she?"

"It's with your Aunt Divine but apparently she's been calling Ms. Lily phone too. Are you sure you are ready for this?"

"Yeah Aunt Pat."

They pull up to a nice roll home in the Overbrook. Pat walks up and rings the doorbell. It took a few seconds but it felt like forever for someone to come to the door. Chante answered the door. She only saw Tiffany maybe twice in her life in person. When she opened the door she seemed to have a little attitude. Lily ordered her to let them in. "Y'all can come in." Chante states as she sucks her teeth. Patricia and Tiffany walk in. A little orange cat rubs up against Tiffany's leg. Lily was sitting in her kitchen peeling potatoes and watching Matlock. "Excuse Chante, she is working my last nerve! Y'all have a seat."

Tiffany studies her grandmother. Her Father kind of looks like his mother but not exactly. She was brown skin with short hair. She seems more active than Grandma Mabel. Like she exercises. "As you know the situation at hand is messed up and I'm not saying I couldn't have reached out but I thought Tiffany was with that horrible woman. I heard from John and he told me to expect your call. It took you long enough so when you called I thought it was about nonsense." Lily explains to Patricia.

"I understand. I appreciate you seeing us."

"Do I call you grandma?" Tiffany blurs out.

"Yes. You are my grandchild. That was your cousin Chante at the door. Your Aunt Divine's daughter. Now that you are old enough you are welcomed to come here. You ain't getting no special treatment. I treat the children the same."

Tiffany didn't know how to feel. She couldn't decide if she was happy or angry. Why didn't she ever see me? Or my Dad for that matter. Lily noticed that Tiffany's mind had drifted off. "Child you alright?"

"Why don't I know you?"

"I'm sorry. I allowed my pride and anger to get in the way of having a relationship with you and my son. Now he's locked up and I told him from the beginning that damn girl was no good." Lily gets up from the kitchen table and opens her arms to Tiffany. "I ask you to forgive me. It doesn't have to be right now, when you're ready. Thank you Pat for bringing her here. I'll be right back. I wanna show you pictures of your family."

Patricia couldn't believe Tiffany was so blunt but she respected it. "Are you okay Tiff?"

"Yes. Are you gonna ask her for Derrick's number while we are here?"

Patricia was again shocked at Tiffany being so blunt. "I wanted you to spend time with your grandma before I went there."

"We ain't time for that. I want my sister safe. We don't know what dumb stuff Brenda has planned. Janelle went by the house for me. It looks abandoned! I'm scared for Vanessa!"

Lily comes back in the kitchen with two photo albums. Lily and Pat switch seats. Lily begins showing her pictures of her Dad when he was younger. Tiffany notices a picture of John and Derrick. " Oh I remember cousin Derrick, Grandma! Where is he? He used to come over all the time!"

"He lives in Virginia now with his family. He got married a few years ago."

"Can I call him?"

"Sure can. I will give you his number. You want your Aunt Divine's number too? I'm sure they would like to hear from you." Lily goes to get her address book out of the living room. Patricia is impressed with how Tiffany was able to get what she needed. "Thank you Tiffany." Pat whispers to Tiffany. Tiffany smiles.

Before the visit was over Tiffany received six birthday cards with money from Lily. Five of the envelopes were all marked with return to sender. Lily explained to Tiffany and Pat she did at one point try to reach out to John but was rejected each time. So she had given up. Tiffany made sure she had given Tiffany her aunt and cousin phone numbers. Lily tells Tiffany next time she will introduce her to Chante properly. Tiffany left her Grandma Lily's house feeling like she found a missing part of herself. She was glad to have helped Aunt Pat so she can help Vanessa. Tiffany misses her siblings so much and is worried about them most of the time. Sometimes she doesn't sleep, it feels like sleeping isn't right if something with Little John or Vanessa.

"Aunt Pat I really don't want to do anything for my birthday tomorrow. I haven't gotten any letters from my Dad. Have you talked to him?"

"No, Tiff. We will be taking that drive to see him again soon. I will ask your Uncle if he's talked to him. Are you sure you don't want a cake? I thought you wanted to see the new Will Smith movie? You know the one with the aliens?"

"It just doesn't feel right to me. I will let you know in the morning." Tiffany went upstairs to her.

July 3, 1996

Tiffany's Birthday

The twins came running in Keke and Tiffany's room with balloons and handmade cards.

"Happy Birthday Tiffany!!" They sang in unison. Tiffany rolled over and saw her two loving twin cousins. She took the balloons and card they got her and hugged them both. "Thank you twins!" Keke woke up and saw the twins jumping around Tiffany. "Happy Birthday Tiff! What are we doing today?"

"I don't know. I might call Janell over to see if Aunt Pat takes us all to the movies to see Independence Day."

"Why Janell gotta come?"

"She's my best friend."

"Oh I see! But when that bitch wasn't around what was I?"

"My best cousin! What is wrong with you?! For your birthday I wasn't even invited! Aunt Pat just brought me along! You were with your high school friends! I didn't trip off that but this is how you do me for my day? And I'm including you!"

"Whatever Tiffany!"

Keke rolled back over and stayed silent. Tiffany decided she wasn't going to let her day be ruined by anyone. Tiffany got up and called Janell. "Hey Tiff Happy Birthday!"

"Thank you...you coming over right? I wanna go to the movies."

"Yes. What time?

"I don't know, I gotta ask Aunt Pat. Just come over as soon as you can. I'm gonna ask her if we can order pizza after the movie. We can have a sleepover kind of thing."

"Ok my Mom will be cool with it." Tiffany and Janell hung up.

I miss Mark. Tiffany knocked on Aunt Pat's bedroom door. She could hear the bed going up and down. Oh wow her and Uncle Jake is nasty. I'm surprised they don't have like ten kids! I'll just come back to her room later.

Tiffany goes back in her bedroom to see Keke up out of bed. She rolls her eyes at Tiffany. "You called Janelle to come over?"

"Yes. I'm waiting on ya nasty ass mom and dad to stop bumping and grinding so I can tell them what I want."

"What do you want?"

"Go to the movies, have pizza, and let Janell sleepover."

"Where is she sleeping? Not in here!"

"Yo why are you acting' this way? We can stay downstairs away from your crazy ass!"

Tiffany got ready to take a shower, on her way to the shower she ran into Aunt Pat who looked extra mellow. "Aunt Pat...can we go to movies, get pizza, and Janell stay the night?"

"Sure." "Happy Birthday Tiffany!" Uncle Jake yelled from the bedroom. Tiffany precedes to the bathroom to take her shower. Before getting in she hears Keke talking shit to Pat. "How come Tiffany gets a sleepover? None of my friends can stay the night?"

"Girl what friends? Those girls you hang around only talk to you because you got money. They aren't your friends. I overheard the one girl from your birthday say how she's jealous of you."

"Whatever Mom! Tiffany gets what she wants!"

"Tiffany don't lie to my face like you do! Or sneak out the damn house! You were lucky to have a damn birthday! You keep that shit up and you're staying home!" Keke stomps back into her room. "Fine I'm not going!" Keke slams the door. Tiffany takes her shower wondering what Keke's problem is?

I loved her and Janell and she shouldn't be jealous. I would meet Keke after school so she could hang with boys. She's always with a different boy. I was shocked when those girls went to Dave and Busters with us. She must really don't have any girls to be friends with. Keke is very pretty though. In our middle school she was friends with this one girl for awhile then she stopped being friends with her too. Now she doesn't want to come to my birthday? Should I make up with her? Tiffany thought to herself. No she should be making up to me! You know what fuck it! Tiffany gets out the shower with her mind made up. She wasn't going to allow anyone to ruin her day.

Tiffany comes downstairs to see Janell sitting on the floor playing with the twins. JJ sure has a crush on Janell. He hugs her every chance he gets and blushes each time. "Happy Birthday Tiffany!!" Janell takes a card out of her back pocket. How thoughtful of Janell.

Everyone went to the movies for Tiffany's birthday, including Keke and Uncle Jake. That made Tiffany very happy. After the movie they went home to have pizza, cake, and ice cream. Pat checked the mail when they got back home and it was an envelope with Tiffany's name on it. Pat gives it to her. Tiffany opens the envelope immediately. It was a birthday card and money from Little John. She shows it to Aunt Pat and Uncle Jake. "That boy is out there. My cop friends don't see him on the corner anymore on Willows. But this is proof that he's still alive." Jake tells Tiffany and Pat as he counts out the money. This time Little John left Tiffany five hundred dollars.

During dinner the telephone rings. Jake picks up the phone. "Tiffany, it's for you." Tiffany gets up to answer the phone, it's her Daddy. Tiffany's heart melts with joy. "Hi Daddy!"

"Happy Birthday Baby! I love you! I can't talk long, but I didn't want to miss your birthday."

"Thank you! I love you too." They hang up. That was the highlight of Tiffany's birthday. JJ was happily sitting next to his Nelly eating pizza. "Do you want more Pepsi Nelly?"

"No thank you JJ." Janelle giggles. Jason doesn't really like how much attention JJ gives Janell. He tried to get JJ to leave the dining room and go play with him. JJ refuses of course. "What's wrong Jason?" Aunt Pat asked. Jason rolls his eyes at Janell. Everyone laughs. Uncle Jake gets up from the table. "Alright I gotta get some rest then be back at work, good night." Everyone said good night except Keke. Keke and Jake haven't talked since he punched her in the chest. Tiffany went into the living room and pulled out all the scariest movies she could think of. "What y'all wanna watch first?" Tiffany is holding 'Child's Play' and 'Nightmare on Elm Street'. Keke and Janell both shrug their shoulders. "You pick it's your birthday!" Aunt Pat yells from the kitchen. Tiffany puts in 'Child's Play.' The girls spend the rest of the night watching scary movies until they fall asleep.

Jay A.K.A
Little John

I had to move out of Skip's house. His daughter was a psycho. She acted like we were supposed to get married or some shit. I almost dimed her out to her mother. All Luz wanted to do was have sex and talk about non sense. I had moves and money to make. So I told Skip I would stay down South Philly with Hazel to keep shit in order. I know when Skip finds out what I have been doing it's going to start a war. I need this move to work. I took over Southwest and South Philly for him and I was ready to branch out. Meeting with Trigger was gonna set everything straight.

Little John has Hazel on board for turning on Skip. Hazel was tired of being Skip's mistress. He promised her months ago that she would run Greenway Avenue and leave his wife. Instead she's been in South Philly taking orders from John and

Major. Ain't nothing like a scorned woman. Jax is dead and turns out he was touchable. Jax had two bad habits that he thought would never come out. He was sleeping with Troy and Veronica. Troy is Jax's bodyguard and secret lover. John had to do a drop to Jax early Sunday morning. He saw through the crack of door Jax sucking Troy off. He waits to knock on the door so they don't suspect that their secret is out. John convinced James to do one more deed. Send word to Troy that Jax was with Veronica. Troy did the deed himself we all know it. John promised James that no one would ever know his involvement and paid him well for it. Nowadays Veronica is hooking up with some New York player almost as if Jax never existed.

Hazel drove them up to the underground Nightclub that Trigger runs. When they entered the club there were two bodyguards standing at the door. A woman came and led them to where Trigger conducted business. Trigger was sitting at his desk waiting patiently for John and Hazel. "Alright let's get to it. You want to give me Southwest and South Philly? That's the word I got from my man Al."

"Yeah that's right. This is Hazel, Skips mistress. She's in on it. We will kill Skip and give you his territory."

"What's in it for you? I heard about you Jay. So I know you up to something…I got more coke than a rich white man can snort. I know you want that! But that ain't all is it?"

"Build with me Trigger. We take out Skip…the war will be brief and small most of Skips soldiers are mistreated. You only need to take out a few. I'll give you where they stay."

Trigger looks at John and Hazel. Something tells Trigger to get on board or he will be dead next. Trigger shakes John and Hazel's hand. "Let's talk about percentages." Trigger states with a laugh.

Brenda

During the spring Brenda reached out to her Aunt Hattie's family in New York. Brenda and Vanessa stayed with Star, Aunt Hattie's daughter. Of course she wheeled them into her web of lies and deceit. She convinced Star to let her daughter Zora come back to Philly with her for the summer. Brenda almost didn't want to return to Philly. The cocaine in New York was way better. Star's boyfriend Victor was a major player in Brooklyn. He would let Brenda sample every time a new shipment arrived. Brenda would happily snort it up with her lucky dollar.

I got reinforcements now. I would take Divine and Zora would take Chante. Brenda is sitting out on the porch smoking a blunt thinking about her plan to attack Divine. While in New York Brenda was calling Lily and Divine's phone making threats to them both on a daily basis. Brenda heard her phone ringing and ran inside. It was Rufus calling from jail again. Rufus is Brenda's cousin on her Dad's side. He's the one stealing Tiffany and John's letters. He works in the mailroom in the prison and is sleeping with one of the Correctional Officers. Rufus has been locked up for almost fifteen years. Rufus is the one Little John heard Brenda on the phone with when Mabel thought she wasn't home. Brenda wanted to make sure she always had one up on John and Tiffany. So far the letters that Rufus has sent her is a bunch of mush. "I got a letter coming to you soon cousin. Something you need to know about ya girl!"

"My girl?"

"Joy!"

"Oh really? Well I look forward to your letter cuz! Don't drop the soap, bye!"

They hang up. Joy huh what the bitch up to? Brenda has put newspapers all over the windows so it looks like no one is home. Brenda has been living mainly in her basement since she came back from New York. Zora and Vanessa stay in the basement with her. It's a fully loaded finished basement with a kitchen area and bathroom. John originally wanted to rent it out, but of course Brenda wasn't having it nor saw the bigger picture. No one knows that Brenda is back except Rufus and that's how she likes it. Fuck all of them! Zora came back from the store with Vanessa. Zora learned her way around quick courtesy of Brenda. She passes for eighteen to buy Brenda's blunts and cigarettes. "Thank you baby girl." Brenda takes the bag that has her food and cigarettes in it. "So when we are going to that bitch house you keep telling me about?"

"Soon..." Brenda takes a drag of her cigarette and zones out. Once I find out what Joy is up to that bitch getting it too.

Jay A.K.A
Little John

John's plan had worked to take out Skips loyal soldiers. The rest fell right in line to his command. Trigger now had control over North, Southwest, and South Philly in a matter of two weeks! Which was all a part of John's plan. No one was safe from this ruthless twelve year old. Tonight Skip dies. Hazel gets out of the car to go to Skips house. Hazel rings the doorbell and Luz comes to the door. "Dad, it's for you! Come in Hazel." Hazel walks in the house to the living room. Skips baby mom notices how sexy Hazel was looking. "What's going on Hazel?"

"I come to talk to you woman to woman before Skip comes down." She looks at Hazel sideways.

"Woman to woman?"

"Yeah I have been fucking Skip for some time now. He promised me that he would leave you! But I see it was all a lie!" Hazel pulls out a black glock with a silencer and points at Skips woman. "Hazel, Skip will be down any minute you won't get away with this!" Hazel shoots her point blank in the face. She falls to the floor. Blood is everywhere. Luz runs out from the dining room to see her mother lifeless in the living room. "Ahh! You bitch!" John comes from behind and grabs Luz. "Where's Skip you dumb bitch!" Luz pees on herself and starts begging John to stop what he's doing. "Please John! I thought you loved me!"

John pushes Luz to Hazel. "Dead her! I'm going upstairs for Skip!" Hazel does as she is told, Luz is dead. John went upstairs. He knew the house too well so he figured Skip would be hiding in the hall closet. Skip pops out the closet but John already has the drop on him. He shoots Skip in the back of the head. Where's Shana? John searches the bedrooms looking for her. He hears crying from under the bed. Found her. John closes the door to make it appear as if he left. Shana comes from under the bed to her death.

Before leaving John opened Skips safe and took out about fifty grand in two of Skips duffle bags. Skip thought he was so much smarter than everyone else. Easy ass safe combination John laughs. Only Skip would make it his birthday! Come on! John laughs to himself and turns the gas on in the kitchen. "Yo Jay chill! Let's go!" Hazel yells. John and Hazel leave Skip's house a bloody mess.

The meet up for after the deed is an abundant house in North Philly. John, Hazel, and the other soldiers are celebrating the new come up. John empties the duffles bags on the table. "My niggas your compensation! If one eating we all eat!" John yells to his crew. "What's next boss?" Angel asked. John was pleased to hear the word 'boss'.

"We let Trigger get comfortable, I'm staying up North with him. Hazel is my right hand; she gets whatever she wants. Stick with me! Don't question me because if you ask, that means Hazel needs to dead you. We took South Philly, we took Southwest and West, North is next. Ya heard me!" John raises his bottle of Mad Dog 20/20 in the air.

Angel understood. He sipped his Bacardi and kept quiet. Who does this boy think he is? How old is he anyway? You can tell he's young but he's built like a football player. Angel curiosity, admiration, and not fully understanding how John could do what he does allowed envy to consume his thoughts. Hazel and John stare at each other. Hazel shoots Angel in the face while he was attempting to take another sip. Everyone stops the celebration. "We can't have that in our circle! You in or you out literally! Now collect the money up and let's bounce!"

Pat

Pat was laying in bed skipping through channels. She stopped at the ten o'clock news to see bodies being shown coming out of a house on Cobbs Creek by the police. "According to neighbors a smell has started coming down the block but no one knew from where. A neighbor noticed that the mother and daughter that lived in the house hadn't been outside in days to have their daily conversations. So she decided to knock on the door and immediately noticed the smell." The reporter tried to get a statement from a police officer but he shot her down. "No comment!" Pat shakes her head. Damn shame. Pat gets up from the bed to check on the children. The twins are sound asleep in their bunk beds. She goes to the girls room. She noticed that Tiffany was swinging her arms while she slept. She went over and began stroking Tiffany's braids until she calmed down and stopped swinging. Pat goes over to Keke's bed and notices that she isn't there. That fuckin' bitch! I can't call Jake, he will kill her. I'm so sick of this with her! Wait until she gets in this house! I don't care if it's the summertime! Patricia goes downstairs and gets her weed from her secret draw. The weed is gone. Now Patricia is furious. She goes and gets a bottle of Mad Dog 20/20 she starts drinking and she hears the front door open slowly. Patricia ducks behind the dining room wall. She waits for Keke to come in the house and start walking up the stairs. Patricia surprises Keke and grabs her down by her hair. Keke screams for mercy but Patricia proceeds to beat on Keke. "Mom stop please!!! I'm pregnant!" Patricia stops and looks at Keke with a busted nose and lip, blood all down her face. She sits on the floor and just cries. Jake's gonna kill her is all that keeps running across Pat's mind. Tiffany and the twins ran down the stairs to see what was going on. Keke was passed out on the floor and Patricia was crying her eyes out. Tiffany runs to the kitchen to get ice for Keke. She instructs the twins to get tissue for their mother's tears. Pat came to her senses and saw that she woke up the house with her actions. Pat tried to wake Keke up from off the floor. Tiffany's ice pack wasn't working. "You are gonna have to help me get Keke in the car!"

"Call the ambulance Aunt Pat!"

"So Jake can find out! No! Help me put her in the van grab her legs!"

Tiffany did as she was told. Pat and Tiffany got Keke in the minivan safely. "I'm taking her to CHOP. Stay here with the twins. I will call you from the hospital, understand?"

"Yeah Aunt Pat." Tiffany went back in the house to the twins.

Pat rushes Keke to the emergency room of CHOP. Keke began to wake up during the car ride. She was able to walk into the hospital. "What are we doing here?" Keke asked.

"You passed out. I want to make sure you and the baby are okay."

When the nurse looked at Pat and Keke she figured the situation was domestic. Keke assured the doctor and nurse that she was not in any danger at home. They performed an ultrasound and Pat saw her grandchild. Keke was ten weeks pregnant, she never started the birth control she prescribed. Pat decided to call Tiffany to let her know everything was okay. "How are the boys?" Pat asked Tiffany.

"They are sleeping. JJ tried to stay up of course. Keke is she okay?"

"She's fine. There's a lot going on. I didn't mean to make you feel like you were back home with Brenda."

"I did for a second while cleaning up the blood. I'm gonna go back to sleep."

"Okay, see you when I get home." Pat hangs up the phone. The nurse explains the discharge instructions to Pat and Keke. Because of Jake being a highly respected firefighter no reports were made.

"You know I have to tell your dad about this." Pat explains to Keke while driving.

"Whatever Mom! I was just keeping cool at the hospital! I'm in love and we are having our baby! His mom said I can come live there too!"

"Bitch make me pull over again and kill you and that baby!"

"You and Dad got pregnant with me! You think I can't do it?"

"Your situation and ours are not the same Keke! Every boy is not your Father! We don't even know anything about him!"

"That's because he's scared of Dad!"

Patricia and Keke go inside the house. "Give me your house keys Keke."

"Why?"

"Because if you leave this house again you won't be able to get back in. You will leave naked because you don't own shit!" Keke looked at her mother and gave Patricia the keys. She went upstairs crying. Patricia went into the dining room to finish that bottle of Mad Dog 20/20.

Jake came home that morning expecting bad news. One of his cop friends who patrols around the hospital told him he thought he saw Pat and Keke. Pat prepared a huge breakfast and made sure the children ate first. The only people at the table were Keke, Jake, and Pat. Jake was eating his pancakes watching his wife and daughter make very little eye contact with each other. Jake sipped his coffee. Pat still barely touched her food. "What is going on? Officer Downs said he saw y'all at the hospital! Keke's face is swollen! What the fuck happened?"

"Babe listen please calm down I will tell you after breakfast." Pat assures.

"Naw forget it! I'm pregnant! Me and Kevin are in love!" Keke shouts.

Tiffany is on the steps ease-dropping. Jake stops eating and calmly says "You're not having it." He proceeds to finish his breakfast. Keke rolled her eyes. "What do you mean?"

"Abortion is what you will be having that's what I mean! I see how I'm gonna have to deal with you Keke."

"Jake, you sure you aren't just upset?" Pat asked with tears coming down her eyes.

"Pat you had one job to take care of kids! You see this shit? Our daughter is fifteen and pregnant! You failed!"

"I failed? Jake we are both her parents! It takes you too! It's a lot out here in this world...we couldn't shelter her!"

"I told you to let me send her ass to an all girl boarding school didn't I?"

"I'm not getting no damn abortion!" Keke shouts getting up from the table. Jake gets up and grabs Keke. "Oh yes you are! Either we go get the abortion or I give you the abortion!" Pat grabs Jake. "Please everyone calm down! Please!"

"I'm going upstairs to bed. Pat called the doctor's office today. I want that baby gone by next week!" Jake goes up the stairs to see Tiffany sitting there in shock. He says nothing and closes his bedroom door.

"Mommy you can't let him do this to me!" Keke cried.

"I'm sorry Keke but you left us no choice." Pat goes in the kitchen to do as she was told. Keke ran upstairs to her room in tears. Tiffany is laying on her bed still in shock of what she heard. "I'm gonna just run away!" Keke is frantic. "Keke your Dad will find you! He got all them cop friends! You're pregnant and you didn't tell me! How did you know?"

"I kept missing my period. I took a test at Kevin house. His family loves me, how my family loves you!" Tiffany looked at Keke. "Wait a minute, you saying this is somehow my fault?" Keke sits on her bed and looks Tiffany straight in the eye. "You think everything is about you don't you? Your mom is fucked up and you took over my room! You come to my school and all the boys like you! No Tiffany this baby is about me! And now if you wasn't here I wouldn't be getting an abortion! You're just another mouth to feed in Jake's eyes." Keke lays down in her bed, she begins to cry. Tiffany gets up and she goes downstairs. Pat is sitting in the living room drinking another bottle of Mad Dog 20/20.

"Aunt Pat are you alright?" Tiffany sits next to her Aunt who appears to be in daze. Pat just burst out screaming. "How could I have been so stupid to think that I could be a mother and wife? I had Keke as a child my damn self! I thought I could trust her to take birth control."

"Aunt Pat, you did your best. Everyone is so jealous of you." Tiffany places her hand in her Aunt's hand. "I love and appreciate you, Aunt Pat." Pat hugs Tiffany. "Thanks Tiffany. I just don't know what we're gonna do with that girl." Pat shakes her head and takes the bottle to her head. Tiffany takes the bottle from her. "Please don't turn into Brenda!"

"Never that. But I will lay off."

August 1, 1996

Brenda Brings the Fight to Divine

Brenda got up with an airtight plan to whoop Divine's ass. Brenda put on a black spaghetti strap shirt and dark blue cut off shorts. Brenda went in her closet upstairs and pulled out her timberland boots. Brenda had Zora put her hair up in a tight bun and she did the same with Zora's hair. Today is payback bitch! My brother been gone a year...cause of that fuckin' John! Brenda is holding back tears as she's deep in her thoughts of how John blew her brothers brains out. Mabel was in the hospital for observation after witnessing the bloody scene created by John. Zora watches Brenda facial expressions. "Yo Brenda? You good?" Zora asked, snapping her fingers.

"Yup. You put your rock sock in ya pocket?" Zora nods yes.

"Grab Vanessa and let's go Brenda stated."

Brenda, Zora, and Vanessa walked to Divine's house which was only fifteen minutes away. The whole time Brenda's blood is boiling. I can't wait to catch Joy's ass next. That bitch been a snitch the whole time! Calling Divine from a pay phone when I was fuckin' Tony! She told John I was fuckin' Derrick! What kind of a best friend was she? Spreading lies on my family! Who does she think she is? What did she want John's pathetic cry baby ass? Oh Divine she disrespected my brothers funeral! All these bitches gonna pay on my brother's soul they're gonna pay!

They got to Divine's house by nine that morning like Brenda planned. She didn't see Dave's car; Divine's husband. Brenda had Zora on look out for the times everyone leaves Divine's house. Brenda sat Vanessa on Divine's next door neighbors steps. "Don't move Ness! You understand?" Vanessa shakes her head yes. Brenda picks up a bottle from the ground and throws it at the indoor porch window. Glass shatters everywhere. You can hear Divine's dog barking. Chante comes to the porch to see glass everywhere. "Mom!!!" Chante yells as she rushes out the house and down the stairs to attack Brenda. "Fuckin' bitch!" Brenda charged back at Chante. The two immediately start punching each other. Zora grabs Chante by her micro braids. "Fight me you dirty bitch!" Zora yelled, punching Chante to the ground. Divine sees her daughter laid out in the street. By this time it's a movie all the neighbors are outside watching and yelling "Damn!" Divine is embarrassed and quickly runs towards Brenda. "Come on Divine!" Brenda yells. Divine runs right into Brenda's sock full of rocks. Divine is stunned. Brenda then hits Divine again with the sock knocking out a piece of Divine's tooth. Divine falls to the ground. Brenda grabs her by the hair. "I hate you! I hate your whole fuckin' family! Y'all killed my brother!" She attempts to hit her again with the sock when the police officer grabs her. "You're under arrest!" Brenda looks and sees the police arresting Zora and another officer placing Vanessa in the car. "What are they doing with my daughter?" Brenda asked the officer as she was being shoved in the car. "No, the question is what are you doing with your daughter that you bring her to a violent scene?"

"Fuck you!"

"You're fucked!" The police officer snaps back at Brenda while driving to the police station. Brenda sits back and closes her eyes. Fuck it, Brenda is thinking. I'll get Mabel to bail me out. I got those dirty bitches good! Divine front teeth are trash now. That will teach Chante to bust my window out! Her ass got laid out hahaha! I got them Todd!

Brenda calls Mabel from the police station.

"What the fuck did you do Brenda?"

"Bail me out! Shit Ma, you know I wasn't gonna let Divine get away with that shit she pulled! And don't get me started on Joy!"

"I'll talk to Sunny. Where's Vanessa and Zora?"

"Child services probably got Vanessa. I don't know what they are doing with Zora but she's gonna be fine. Bail me out and come get my baby!"

"I'm calling Pat to get Vanessa! I'm not coming up anywhere!"

"Mom-" Mabel hung up on Brenda. Fuck not Pat! Brenda goes back to her holding cell mad as hell. Damn it! I didn't plan that part out right! If Little John was home he would've had her. Pat is going to try to take my baby. I know she is! A woman is sitting next to Brenda on the bench. "You got a cigarette beautiful?" Brenda shakes her head no and goes back into her thoughts. I gave her Tiffany that was easy fuckin' disgusting daughter of mine. Seducing my brother what kind of a girl does that to her own uncle? But Pat wasn't getting Vanessa!

Pat

Pat is on the phone talking to Jake about the twins day at camp when her other line clicks. "Hold on Jake." She clicks over. "Hello?"

"It's your mother Mabel. This is an emergency. I just got off the phone with Star and she told me that Brenda and Zora got locked up and had Vanessa with them! Brenda called me because she wanted me to get her out. You need to get Vanessa cause I'm sure DHS got her at this point."

"Wait a minute why is Zora and Brenda locked up to begin with?"

"She went to Divine house! Brenda ain't making bail she got a prior warrant out for shoplifting. She knocked Divine teeth out! Go get my grand baby and ask for Cecil Dexter down at DHS." Pat forgot all about Jake being on the other line. "Hold on Mabel." Pat tells Jake she will call him back. "Yeah so when did this happen?"

"Thursday. Sunny is getting Brenda a lawyer because she is looking at a mandatory 1 year sentencing and probation. He got a lawyer that can cut all that in half he said."

"I don't care about Brenda being locked up! It's Saturday and you just now calling me to get Vanessa? Typical Mabel. Bye." Brenda hung up the phone. "Tiffany!"

Tiffany comes into the bedroom dressed up. "Where are you going?"

"Mark is out! His uncle came to get me and we went to a restaurant called Old Country Buffet. I was gonna tell you but you were on the phone, so I waited."

"Brenda got locked up with your cousin Zora from New York. She beat up your Aunt Divine and cousin Chante."

"Where is Vanessa?"

"I'm about to call DHS and find out."

"When can we see my dad again? I haven't gotten any letters. I'm worried! Do you want me to stay home?"

"No go have fun with Mark and his Uncle. You know if he does one more stupid thing you can't see him anymore."

"He learned his lesson, Aunt Pat. When I come home will Vanessa be here?"

"That's the plan. I'm gonna get ya uncle to pull some strings."
Tiffany leaves the room. Pat gets on the phone to call Jake.
"Hello."

"Babe are you still friends with Krystal?"

"Yeah why? Vanessa is in DHS. I wanna get her today like now."

"Get the fuck outta here! I'm gonna make a few calls...give me a couple of hours, I'll call you back." Pat and Jake hang up. Pat decides to go to the girls room and check on Keke. "Ke, I want you to know that I'm gonna go get your little cousin Vanessa."

Keke rolls her eyes and turns over. "Why are you telling me? Tiffany's whole family is gonna live here? But I had to kill my baby?" This what Pat has been dealing with since the abortion. Tiffany started sleeping on the pull out couch in the living room. Kevin broke up with Keke so she couldn't run away there like she originally planned. "Keke I can't take back what happened but you were given birth control for a reason. Now you gotta get a shot every three months and you can't ditch that. You put this on yourself. Tiffany didn't ask for her circumstances."

That evening...

As promised to Tiffany, Vanessa was sitting in the living room playing with the twins happily. Pat decided to cook fried chicken, mashed potatoes, and collard greens. Pat called the children to the table. "Keke!" Pat yelled up the stairs. No answer. "Keke get ya ass downstairs!" No answer. "JJ go get ya sister out of her room." JJ goes to do as he's told. A few moments later JJ yells down the stairs. "Mommy Keke won't get up!" Pat runs up the stairs frustrated. Here she goes with her shit. Pat goes into the room and sees her daughter passed out on the bed with a bottle of Tylenol next to her. She smacks Keke several times in the face. No response. She feels a weak pulse. Pat calls 911 with no hesitation. Oh my God my daughter! Tears are flowing down Pat's eyes. "Mommy why are you crying? What's wrong with Keke?"

The ambulance came and rushed Keke back to Children's Hospital. Keke's stomach was pumped to remove all the Tylenol from her system. Jake arrives at the hospital. "Pat what the fuck?!?" Jake screams.

"I don't know she must have taken them when I left to get Vanessa! She didn't want to go with me!" Pat cried. Jake started punching the hospital wall. "Sir! You can't do that here!" The security guard states as he gets from his desk to approach Jake. "Fuck!" Jake kept screaming. The twins and Vanessa just stared at the two adults losing their minds right before their eyes. The doctor comes out to them. "Listen, Keke is stable. We recommend therapy. She suffered the loss of her baby. She's depressed." Jake looked at the doctor. "I don't want her home until she's better ya understand? Ok Doc!"

"Please forgive him. We had to make a choice that led us here. Keke wasn't taking her birth control. We have a house full." Pat explains everything to the doctor. She seemed to understand and now just like Tiffany did for the rest of the summer Keke will be staying at Children's Hospital.

Tiffany

Since Keke ain't here I have been sleeping in my bed. She really lost her mind. She blames me for her choices she made. I wish my mom was Aunt Pat. All she does is take care of everything and everyone. Keke is stupid she has no idea how good she has it, compared to me. Mark has been different but in a good way. His uncle put him in a private school. He's friends with the director so now Mark gotta wear a uniform. I can't believe my baby is a junior and I'm a freshman. I really don't like school. I promised Aunt Pat to do my best and not get into trouble. It's a good thing me and Janell are going to Bartram together. So I won't be alone. I get to be with my baby sister. I missed Vanessa so much she got so big. She talks a lot too. Vanessa told Tiffany about Brenda putting white powder up her nose with money, her trip to New York, fighting Divine, and anything else Tiffany wanted to know.

I'm glad DHS finally caught up Brenda's ass is all Tiffany kept thinking. "Tiff she said your daddy not my daddy! Who is my dad then?" Vanessa asked while practicing writing her name. Unfortunately due to Brenda's parenting skills Vanessa is behind for a six year old. Brenda stopped taking her to school. Tiffany looked at Vanessa. I gotta tell Aunt Pat to call Derrick ain't no need in sugarcoating this shit any longer. "Nessa I know who ya daddy is but it's a secret right now!"

"Ooo a secret! Ok, you gonna surprise me?"

"Uh huh big surprise!" Tiffany hugged Vanessa tight. Tiffany told Nessa to continue practicing writing her name. She was catching on fast which made Tiffany happy. No one wanted a dumb little sister.

Tiffany went downstairs to the kitchen, Aunt Pat was making a seafood pasta salad for dinner. "What's up Tiffany? You are making one of your famous faces!"

"Brenda told Ness that my dad isn't her dad and she asked me who her dad is."

Pat stopped mixing the pasta salad. "You fuckin' with me right?"

"I wish..."

"You know I have been delaying that call. I guess I ain't got a choice now."

"Nope! So...you getting Keke tomorrow?"

"Yeah. They wouldn't let her have phone calls like that since she was on suicide watch. We will see what happens. You gonna try and stay in the room?"

"I will see. I don't want any problems since Vanessa is sleeping with me. She sounds like she hated everybody in the house."

The phone rings with a similar number to John. Tiffany answers it thinking it's her dad.

"Yes I accept!" Tiffany says happily not fully listening to the props.

"Hey Tiff it's ya mother." Tiffany looks at the phone with disappointment. "Brenda? What do you want?"

"I wanna see my girls. Let me speak to Pat, please."

This the most sober she has ever heard Brenda sound in her entire life. Tiffany passes the phone to Pat. "Hello?"

"Pat it's Brenda. Can you please bring me my daughters. I wanna see them. I miss y'all."

"Brenda you for real?"

"Yeah. I'm for real. I called Derrick too. So look out for his call okay. He is going to get DNA tested for Nessa. The papers are gonna come in the mail to your house soon."

Pat couldn't believe what she was hearing. "Give me your information. I will bring the girls this week. Tiffany starts high school next week."

"Wow. Damn look at how time flies." Brenda gave Pat her information, she had already put everyone on the visiting list. Tiffany looked at Pat in such disbelief. "Was that really Brenda?" Tiffany started picking at her braids. Pat grabs Tiffany's arm to stop her from pulling her hair. "Yeah Tiffany. I understand what you may be thinking but we are going. She already spoke to Derrick."

"How do you know she ain't lying?"

"We don't! So we are going to make sure we look good on our end. She clearly is clean and sober so a part of her has to be thinking straight."

"I want to see my dad!"

"This weekend, okay. You know I had to get the van tuned up for that long ride. So this week you will see both ya parents. Now let me put this in the fridge for a few hours then we can eat."

Tiffany got on the phone upstairs in Aunt Pat's room to call Mark. He gotta know about this shit. Before she could make the call JJ announces Janell is here. I'll call him later. Tiffany ran downstairs to her B.F.F. "Nell we gotta talk outside! Let's go to the gallery for a little bit. I still got some birthday money." The two leave the house and walk to the 34 trolley. Janell is curious to what's going on. She knows Keke is bat shit crazy. But what new shit is Tiffany about to tell her?

"My mom called from jail saying she wanna see me and Vanessa!"

"What!"

"Yes Janell! I'm gonna see my dad this weekend too! I still haven't gotten a letter from him either!"

"It's hard for him in jail. You will be okay once you see him. I wanna go to City Blue and see what sneakers they got."

"Okay. My aunt made a seafood salad. I wanna eat that so I'm only getting a milkshake from McDonalds."

Tiffany and Janell enjoyed their time downtown. Of course teenage boys eyed them down and wanted their attention. Janell wrote down a few numbers she liked. Tiffany was too stuck on Mark to take a new number. On the way home Tiffany told Janell how Brenda got locked up and who Vanessa's dad really was. "Girl your life is like Jerry Springer!"

"Tell me about it! And you Keke's crazy ass come home tomorrow. I'm staying out her way for real! She doesn't listen to anybody!"

Tiffany visit's Brenda in Jail

Tiffany couldn't believe how clean Brenda looked. She probably gained a good ten pounds. Vanessa was happy to see her mommy. She ran up to her with open arms. Pat and Brenda gave each other a pat on the back. Tiffany just said "hello." Everyone sat at the table in silence for a good minute before Pat sparked a conversation. "How are you Brenda?"

"I'm clean shit! They are strict in this bitch! You know Uncle Sunny hooked me up with a bomb ass lawyer. He paid up the house for me too! So when I come home I can have my girls! Ha!"

Tiffany rolled her eyes. Vanessa screamed "Yay Mommy!" Pat noticed Tiffany's attitude. "You alright?" Tiffany sighed heavily.

"Oh Tiff! Baby I'm gonna do right okay. I forgive you for what you did." Tiffany thought about ripping Brenda's head off. "Bitch are you serious? What did I did? I asked your brother to rape me?" Vanessa started crying. Brenda decided to remain calm; she didn't want to ruin her chances of getting out of prison in the winter. "You don't know what it was like growing up with Mabel!" Brenda tried to explain but Tiffany didn't care she got up from the table. "No I don't but I know what it was like growing up with you! I hate you Brenda! I don't care if I ever see you again! I want to leave now Aunt Pat! Why did you bring me here!" Tiffany started shaking and crying. "I wanna kill her!" Pat got up from the table and took Vanessa with her. "Brenda we gotta go..." Brenda left the table immediately never once looking back.

"Tiffany I'm sorry I brought you here!" Pat tells Tiffany as they get in the van. Tiffany was able to calm Vanessa down into a nap. She had to carry her to the car. "What made you think she was cool? For real though? She ain't never changing! Vanessa is too young to understand. She will get over it." Tiffany looks out the window doing her best to block out this visit to see Satan. "I don't know...I mean Keke came home happy and healthy. I thought Brenda was getting on track. I was wrong." The entire ride home was silent.

John's Revenge

John would see all the other inmates receive their mail with no problem. So he asked the C.O. that was friends with Jake to investigate the matter. He told John how Rufus is sleeping with Justin the correctional officer, he saw Rufus opening mail. John couldn't figure out why this guy would steal his mail so he asked correctional officer Linden, Jake's friend, to set up a one-on -one with Rufus. Officer Linden pretended to make a pass at sweet ass Rufus, he fell right into the trap.

John waited for Rufus in the linen area after hours. "Oh officer Linden! Where are you at Boo?" Rufus sings as he sees a shadow in the corner. "This isn't officer Linden...It's John and I want to know why you are stealing my mail?" John grabs Rufus by the throat and places him up against the wall, he puts a jailhouse shank to Rufus' head. Rufus is petrified. "Aww! John? I don't know what you're talking about!" John places the blade down Rufus face lightly. "Oh you don't? Why am I the only one not receiving my letters? Now you answer wrong next time and I'm gonna jab this blade straight into your head!" John squeezes Rufus throat tighter to let him know he means business before lightening up his grip. "Okay okay...so...I did it for my cousin! You killed my cousin!" Rufus tried to give John a body shot with his fist but failed miserably. "You kin to that son of bitch Todd? You took my letters for Brenda?" John loses it. He stabs Rufus over and over again until there is no Rufus to identify. Blood is all over the white linens. Blood is all over John's hands. He hurries up to take the shank out of Rufus' left eye. John rushes to his cell to clean himself as best as possible.

Jake gives Pat the Bad News

Pat is helping Vanessa and the twins practicing writing their ABC's when Jake calls. "Hey baby!" Pat answers happily.

"You sitting down?"

"Yeah I'm with the kids."

"Go in the other room." Pat goes in the kitchen with her heart pounding.

"What is it? I'm in the kitchen."

"John killed somebody in prison."

"What!"

"He killed Brenda's cousin Rufus...Rufus was taking the mail. John was put in the hole. No visits. You gotta tell Tiffany. I'm sorry, when I get more info I'll let y'all know. Damn it that fuckin' Brenda!" Jake hangs up the phone with disgust. Pat sits in the dining room at the table feeling stupid. Why did I believe that Brenda was gonna be a better person? At least she didn't lie about the DNA test for Vanessa. I gotta take Vanessa next week. But what's this bitch motive? Now I gotta tell Tiffany she can't see her dad before school starts. How to tell her? Should I cook a big meal? No. She already knows that means bad news. How do I tell her this? Pat decided to take Tiffany to the Old Country Buffet. She likes it there. Poor girl.

Pat asks Keke to watch the children while she steps out with Tiffany. Since Keke had been on meditation she seems better. They had to hide all the medications and belts in the house. Keke hasn't shown any signs of suicide so Pat felt confident to leave her with the kids.

"Come on Tiff let's go for a ride." Pat and Tiffany get in the van. Tiffany is excited about the unexpected day out. She had been feeling nervous about high school next week. "Where are we going?"

"To Old Country Buffet!"

Tiffany's face lit up with joy. "For real! Just me and you!"

"Yup just us! Thought this would cheer you up from seeing Brenda."

"I can't wait to see my Daddy!"

"Uh huh" Pat cuts on the radio. Tiffany is content with the music. The ride was smooth.

Pat waited for them to start eating before spilling the bad news to Tiffany. "I gotta tell you something Tiffany. I didn't know how to say it at home so I figured I'll tell you here."

Tiffany stops eating her slice of pizza. "What?"

"You can't see your dad this weekend. Something happened."

Tiffany's heart sunk to the floor. "What? Is he hurt?"

"No. He hurt someone and now he's in the hole. He can't have visitors."

"Somebody was messing with him huh? My daddy doesn't play!"

"I'm glad you're taking it well."

"Are you telling me everything? I can take it Aunt Pat. You seem like you are missing something."

"He killed Rufus, Brenda's cousin…apparently he's the one who was stealing the mail."

"What! I don't know him but if he was doing that then Brenda knew about it! That bitch!! You thought she was being good!"

"I know Tiffany. I'm so sorry! I know you wanted to see your father in a couple of days."

"It's okay. I understand. I'm glad he handled that. Now I can write my Daddy letters once he gets out of the hole. Tiffany and Pat ate so much food. The day out turned out better than Pat thought it would. The aunt and niece then walked the Springfield Mall. Tiffany was a little bit disappointed that she wouldn't see her dad. Tiffany was content with knowing that her father was a fighter.

Tiffany

It was my first day of high school and I could barely sleep, I stayed up on the phone with Mark most of the night. I decided to wear light blue jeans, an orange polo shirt, and white keds. Keke did not look thrilled about returning to Bok. She overheard Keke begging Pat to switch her out because she didn't want to see Kevin. "You will be alright Keke. You might not see him anyway, he's in the twelfth grade now right?" Keke didn't answer her, she walked out the room. Well fuck giving words of advice Pat.

Aunt Pat gave us a ride to school. The twins were excited about school as well, Vanessa couldn't start school yet. Aunt Pat wanted to wait for the DNA test to come back. I eavesdropped on Aunt Pat and Derrick's phone conversation. He said if Vanessa is his she's going to Virginia with him. A judge would grant him full custody with no problem because of Brenda's record. I was going to miss Vanessa. We have had so much big sister and little sister time. Vanessa can read and write better. The only thing I get from Little John is money left in the mailbox. At least I know he's alive though. This weekend he left one thousand dollars. Aunt Pat said we couldn't tell Uncle Jake about it.

"Tiffany and Janell y'all ready?" Aunt Pat asked as she pulled up to Bartram High School.

"Yeah. I guess." Tiffany and Janell got out of the van looking at how big the building was. Tiffany noticed a few familiar faces from both middle schools. Aw shit she's here great. Tiffany points to Rhonda and her corny crew. Janell laughs. "Oh shit ain't seen here since we beat that ass in seventh grade!"

Rhonda and her crew walked by and rolled their eyes at them. Tiffany decided to just laugh it off. She promised Aunt Pat no trouble. Tiffany and Janell had all the same classes together which made the transition into high school much easier for them both. At lunch they went outside to the corner store to get cheesesteaks and sodas. "Do you wanna ditch? We have not learned anything yet." Janell asked while they ate lunch in a back hallway. "Naw let's stick it out. I'm gonna meet Mark downtown afterwards. You wanna come he said he gonna bring you some niggas."

"I'm down."

The first day of high school was a blur to Tiffany all she cared about was seeing Mark. They all met up at McDonalds as promised and he brought two boys from his old high school for Janell to choose from. Tiffany and Mark hugged each other. "You look different in that uniform yo!" Tiffany tells Mark as she kisses his neck. She sits on his lap at the table inside McDonalds. "Shut up Tiffany! Are you coming over this weekend?"

"Yeah."

"My uncle is leaving Friday night for business. He won't be back until Sunday."

"Ooo I got an idea Tiffany!" Janell yells in between flirting with both boys.

"Say you are spending the night at my grandma house with me so you can be at Mark house all weekend."

"Okay you on it." Tiffany gives Janell a pound.

When Tiffany got home she went to Aunt Pat's room. The door was closed so she knocked. Do I smell weed? "Aunt Pat..." Tiffany hears Aunt Pat spraying. Oh shit Aunt Pat is getting high, Tiffany laughed to herself. Pat opens the door and then hurries to her bed to lay down so Tiffany can't see her high. "Can I spend the night at Janell grandma house on Friday?"

"Sure. Have fun." Tiffany is relieved. That was easy. She closes her door. Tiffany goes downstairs to the kitchen to call

Mark and let him know the plan is on. Tiffany is so thrilled. Janell is so smart! Tiffany stays downstairs with Vanessa to watch cartoons. Keke comes into the house with an attitude. "I saw Kevin! He told the boys not to talk to me! He said I'm a murderer!" Keke starts crying hysterically. "I told her to transfer me! I told her!" Tiffany feels helpless. She just watches Keke fall to the floor kicking and screaming. Pat hears all the commotion, she comes downstairs to see her daughter in a fit. "What is going on?" Pat asks.

"I told you to transfer me! You ruined my life! Kevin told people I'm a murderer! I hate y'all!"

Pat tried to console her traumatized daughter. We should have just let her have that damn baby. Jake just wouldn't have it Pat thought to herself. "I'll talk to your dad Keke. I'm sorry you had to go through that." Keke cries herself to sleep on the floor in her mother's arms. Tiffany and Vanessa continue to watch Cartoon Network not saying a word.

Tiffany stayed downstairs that night with Vanessa, she didn't want to be near Keke in that state of mind.

The weekend came fast just as Tiffany hoped. She got home from school and packed her bags to Mark's house. She was in for a about a two hour septa ride but she didn't care. Before she left the house she had Janell meet her at the house so that Aunt Pat wouldn't get suspicious. "See you Sunday Janell!" They hugged each other at the trolley stop and went there separate ways. The whole ride to Mark's house all Tiffany thought about was her Father. I wonder how long he is going to be in the hole? I don't want to send any letters off until I know he can get them. That bitch Brenda and her corny ass cousin Rufus. Who the fuck is he anyway?

Tiffany was so excited to get to Mark's house. As soon as he opened the door Tiffany jumped on him. "Hey Tiffany! I miss you too. I wanna do something different."

"What?"

"My uncle got a new shower. You wanna do it in the shower?"

"Hell yeah."

Tiffany and Mark had continuous sex through out the house. It was around one in the morning when the two fell asleep.

That Saturday morning Tiffany attempted to make pancakes and eggs. She burnt three pancakes before getting it right. Mark sat at the kitchen table watching her and laughing at Tiffany's cooking skills. "Shut up Mark! I don't cook at home! My Aunt makes it look so easy!" Once she was finished they had breakfast. "Do you want to go to Franklin Mills?"

"Okay." The phone rings. Mark answers it while eating a pancake with his hand.

"Yeah." Mark is quiet for the first two minutes of being on the phone then he replies. "Naw not today my girl is here. I'll catch up with you later." Mark hangs up the phone and sits back at the table. "Who was that?" Tiffany asked while rolling her eyes. "My neighbor Cathy who plays ball."

"Cathy? What kind of a name is that?!"

"Don't start Tiffany. She's a white girl. She lives across the street. We play ball sometimes. It ain't about nothing."

"It better not be. Cause I'll beat y'all ass!"

Mark gives Tiffany a kiss on the cheek. "You always wanna fight somebody!"

Tiffany and Mark went out to the Franklin Mills Mall and forgot all about Cathy.

Brenda

When Brenda got the word from Mabel that Rufus was dead. She lost her mind. I tried to forgive and forget while locked up I truly did. But now I see there's no point. John killed my brother and Rufus. How did he find out? Rufus must've slipped up. I don't have any pull now. Fuck it all! Derrick is gonna take Vanessa from me! The Judge ruled him full custody. They all tricked me! Once I get out of here I'm gonna find a way to kill John! I swear it. Oh don't think I haven't forgotten about Joy ass. Who knows what kind of letters she is sending John now that Rufus is dead. I wonder if Victor got any pull in John's jail. Brenda calls Mabel to give Star a message. Even though Brenda got Zora locked up in the juvenile detention center for a month there was no bad blood. Star was just as grimy as Brenda. In New York Star would get Zora to handle girls on a weekly basis to fight. Star and

Brenda got high together her entire trip to New York. Now

Brenda was itching for cocaine more than ever. Brenda

planned to make nice while in jail and countdown the days to

February 5, 1997.

Brenda goes back to her cell happily plotting her revenge on

John.

October 5, 1996

Derrick takes Vanessa

Derrick told Pat he would be up to Philadelphia on Saturday with his wife and their daughter Vivian. Vivian is four years old. As soon as she saw Vanessa and the twins she greeted them and immediately made herself at home. "Why do you talk like that?" JJ asked Vivian. "Huh?" Vivian says smashing play dough. Pat signals JJ to behave. The children had never heard a southern accent before. Derrick and his wife Theresa sat down at the dining room table. Pat prepared a large early dinner for everyone. Fried chicken, fried flounder, baked macaroni and cheese, collard greens, string beans, potato salad, and cornbread. Tiffany sat at the table in disbelief that today would be the last day she sees her baby sister, unless they take a six hour drive to Virginia. Jake made sure he was present for this day. Keke barely said a word but had been in better spirits. She was still attending Bok but something else now had her attention. "I haven't seen you Tiffany in so long. You have grown so much." Derrick begins eating his dinner happily. Theresa looks around at everyone, she was grateful for the hospitality that was being displayed. When Derrick explained to Theresa about Vanessa at first she was not pleased. However she is in love with the man she married and was not going to hold his past against him. "Have y'all explained to Vanessa that she is coming with us?" Theresa asked. "No not exactly. We told her we are gonna surprise her with who her Daddy is." Tiffany replied. "So how does she know John is not her father?" Theresa asked. Theresa realized she had a lot of questions. "Brenda told her." Pat answers.

"We think it's best if you, Derrick talk to her." Jake explains while shoveling potato salad down his throat. Derrick agrees. I can't believe my past came back to bite me in ass Derrick says to himself. "I was a horrible cousin and friend to John. He didn't deserve that." Derrick began pouring his heart out at the table. "Brenda and I started doing coke together. John didn't party. I felt like because she was my cousin's wife it was all good. Then one thing led to another and now here's Vanessa." Jake pats Derrick on the back. "I ran off instead of facing my responsibilities. John told me he was having marital problems like he knew it was me."

"Derrick, he did know. Because Joy told." Pat blurs out.

"Joy? She was partying with us! We all had a three-" Derrick watches his words he almost forgot there were children present.

"We get the picture." Jake tells Derrick. Tiffany stopped eating when she heard that part. Wow Joy ain't shit either. Derrick and Theresa take Vanessa into the living room to explain who he is and that she will be living with them. Everyone remains quiet in the dining room so they can hear as best as possible. "Vanessa I'm your dad. This is my wife

Theresa and we want you to come live with us in Virginia."

Vanessa turns her head to the dining room. "Is Tiffany coming?" Tiffany goes into the living room. "No but I'm gonna come visit. You're now a big sister! Vivian is your baby sister." Vanessa gets excited about being a big sister. "Okay are you rich? My mom said my real dad rich." Derrick laughs off the question. That damn Brenda. She must have heard I won the lottery a while back. Whose business don't this bitch know? That's why she wanted to do the DNA test! She thought I was gonna be paying out the ass in child support! Clever ass Brenda, I gotta hand it to her. Derrick assures Vanessa that they are "rich" enough.

Vanessa waves goodbye to everyone happily. Theresa told her that they will go to Chuck E. Cheese tomorrow in Virginia. Vanessa has no idea what Virginia is, she is just excited to have a rich dad and baby sister. Pat and Jake couldn't believe how easy that went. They were for sure that Vanessa would go kicking and screaming. Tiffany however went upstairs to cry in the bathroom. She didn't know if she was happy or sad that Vanessa was getting a new life. Why couldn't she stay here? Maybe it's for the best? Maybe not? Is Derrick rich? Why would Brenda tell Vanessa that? She had to know something! Tiffany wipes her face and goes back downstairs. "Is Derrick rich?" Tiffany asked her Aunt and Uncle. "Word is he hit the lotto awhile back and that's why he moved to VA." Pat explains to Tiffany. "Is that right. So Vanessa is set then? Brenda wanted Vanessa to be better off?"

"It's Brenda Tiffany! She probably thought she was gonna get mad child support. Jokes on her ass!" Pat starts laughing hard. The twins start laughing with her. Keke and Jake just stare. Tiffany giggles and realizes that Vanessa leaving was indeed for the best.

January 1997

Tiffany

Thanksgiving, Christmas, and New Years came and went for Tiffany. All she could think of was her dad. Still no letter or phone call from him. Uncle Jake assured Tiffany that he was safe. For Christmas Little John left in the mailbox two thousand dollars. Tiffany didn't show Aunt Pat all that money. Tiffany started noticing Little John's pattern and would start checking the mailbox all week before Christmas. She gave her Aunt Pat two hundred dollars. "Please give all of it to my dad Aunt Pat." Tiffany decided to start saving money for herself. So she hid it in the floorboard of her room. Just in case I have to find my own way. She noticed that Aunt Pat was getting comfortable with Little John's street money. Whatever Uncle Jake gives her must not be enough. I don't want her thinking she can have all the money and only give me what she wants me to have. I mean I got a few new outfits but I need a new coat and Tims. I'll just lie and say Mark brought me new things. It's not unusual for him to buy me things. I just wish I could see Vanessa and Little John. Little John was gonna be turning thirteen February 1ˢᵗ. He probably doesn't even care all the money he seems to have. I tried to ask him about a corner boy who looked at me sideways. "Move along shawty! I don't know no Little John!"

I'm glad that Vanessa at least calls. She is starting to sound like she's from down south. Derrick and Theresa are definitely spoiling those girls. "Tiffany, me and my little sister got Barbie bikes! I got new shoes too! When are you coming to see me?" That's all Vanessa does is tell Tiffany what her and Vivian received and asks when she is coming to visit. Vanessa told Tiffany to hurry up to her because they are going to see Mickey Mouse soon.

Tiffany had noticed that Keke started acting like her old self. She started joining Tiffany and Janell watching videos and girl gossip. Keke started smiling more. So Tiffany decided to ask her before bed what was up. "Keke you all regular again what's up?"

Keke turned over in her bed. "I met a man girl! His name is Tommy. He's twenty and he got dough! I was crying at the bus stop and he saw me. He pulled over and started talking to me. I told him about Kevin's ass. Girl, he took care of Kevin too!" Tiffany went over to Keke's bed. "What do you mean took care of?" Keke smiled. "He got his bulls to fuck him up! I watched in Tommy's car. Kevin don't bother me anymore nobody at the school does!" Tiffany never thought Keke had street in her. Now I know why she's been so happy. "When do you see Tommy?" Tiffany at this point was curious. Keke is messing with a twenty year old! "Everyday. Sometimes I don't go to school. He picks me up and takes me around the way to his house."

"Where does he live?"

"South Philly. He is a drug dealer though so he leaves and comes back. I just chill in the house with his cousins."

"Girl are you crazy? You better hope ya dad don't find out!"

"Fuck my mom and dad. I can live with him."

"Keke I'm going to bed. You are a crazy girl."

The next morning Tiffany woke up a few minutes to catch Keke leaving out so she could see who this 'Tommy' is. She looked out the window to see Keke walk to the corner of the block and turn. Shit they are smart! I tried to be so fuckin' nosy! Tiffany hears the phone ring. It's only 6:45 in the morning who could be calling so early? All she hears is Aunt Pat's piercing screams "Noooo! Noooo! Oh God No!" Tiffany rushes in to her Aunt who still has the phone in her hand screaming and crying. "What's going on?"

"It's Jake! It's Jake! I gotta get to the hospital. His job said he was in a horrible fire! Did Keke leave out for school?"

"Yes, you want me to stay home and take the twins to school?"

Pat immediately threw on whatever she had on her bedroom floor. She didn't even answer Tiffany. Tiffany heard the twins waking up in their room so she went in there to keep them from coming out seeing their mother in the state she was in. Once Tiffany heard the front door slam she brought the twins out so they could eat breakfast.

Jake's End

Jake didn't think that was the last time he would suit up for being a Philadelphia Firefighter. Jake never thought that he would never see his family again. To Jake it was another row home fire in Southwest Philadelphia. It's cold so the use of ovens and heaters at night are at a high. So when they received the call to report to 57th and Windsor, Jake figured business as usual. Once Jake arrived at the scene three homes were on fire plus one house was reported to have four dead bodies in it that initially started the fire. That house burnt down completely. The news channels were already on the scene calling it a homicide arson. Jake's team was in charge of the second house that was on fire. Taming the fire was going well at first. Until Jake faintly hears a elderly lady yelling that she was trapped in the bathroom from the side of the house. "The window can only open halfway!" The lady explained. "I'm going up!" Jake yelled. "No! Jake don't go in it's a suicide mission! The house is falling apart!" Jake goes against his team members' advice. The firefighters did their best to keep the fires down from the second and third house. The third house only had a woman and child inside who made it out safely. The elderly woman lived alone and she tried to escape the fire as best she could. When Jake got inside the house smoke and flames were everywhere. The house was unkempt. The hardwood floors were falling apart. Jake ran up the stairs as fast as he could. He fell at the last step cracking his face mask. Smoke began filling into his lungs. Jake was able to make it to the elderly woman in the bathroom. Her right leg was severely burned. Jake tried to carry her but the floors began to collapse. Jake and the elderly woman fell into the dining room from the second floor.

When Pat arrived at the hospital and saw her husband burnt beyond recognition she lost it all over again. His teammates tried to console her but failed. "Oh my God! Jake! Jake!"

The doctor comes into the room to deliver an update. "We are just keeping him comfortable there is nothing we can do. It's up to you to pull the plug. I'm sorry." Pat starts to cry uncontrollably. Jake has a little family. His grandmother passed away ten years ago. Jake's parents may or may not be alive. The only person she knew to contact was his Aunt Sarah, his mother's sister. Pat wasn't in any condition to call anyone but she did so anyway, sounding hysterical on the phone she was able to contact Aunt Sarah. "I'll be there as fast as I can Pat!" Pat thought of the children wondering rather or not to bring them there. No they can't remember him like this! Why is this happening to me? Why now? What did I do to deserve this? Is it because of Keke's abortion? Pat sits in the chair next to Jake's bed crying her heart out. Aunt Sarah arrives with a few other relatives Pat never met. "We are ready now." Pat tells the doctor. The plug is pulled on Jake. He dies instantly after.

That late afternoon...

After Pat pulled the plug on her lifeless husband, Jake's family followed her back to the house to tell the children the horrible news. Tiffany kept the twins home with her waiting patiently for a phone call from her Aunt Pat she never received. When Tiffany saw everyone coming in she feared the worst. "Aunt Pat, what's going on? You never called! Who are these people?" Pat told Tiffany to bring the twins down to the living room. "Yo Mommy!" The twins yelled in unison. "Where's Keke?" Pat asked Tiffany. "She ain't here yet." Pat shook her head. I'll deal with her later. "Everyone please go to the dining room." Pat instructs everyone. Tiffany and the twins follow everyone into the dining room.

"I thank you for coming. I need to know where Jake's parents are?" Pat asked.

"My sister is still alive, she's locked up. Jake's daddy died in jail. It was a big riot." Aunt Sarah answers. Pat felt some relief. I wonder if Jake ever knew that? Tiffany sat at the dining room table putting together that Uncle Jake was gone. Tears started flowing down her eyes. "Tiffany, why are you crying?" JJ asked. "Nothing. Y'all come on upstairs with me. Let's play uno." The twins follow Tiffany back upstairs. Pat puts her head down into her arms. Jake's cousin Simone tries to lighten the mood. "We were proud of Jake and his family. He kept in contact with me here and there. We kind of fell out of touch when I moved to Atlanta for a while. We just got back in touch with each other and we planned on getting together soon so I could meet you and the kids."

"I'm Simone's brother Charles. I was in the service a long while."

"These are my children." Aunt Sarah explains to Pat. Aunt Sarah is older than Jake's mother Claire. Claire has been in prison since Jake was three years old. Her and Jake's father were both sentenced to life in prison by the state of Pennsylvania. They had been robbing banks in the county for about two years. Their last bank robbery ended with a high speed chase and two civilians dead. Trudy raised her girls as best as she could. Claire always had been on the wild style. Aunt Sarah felt it was her duty to pick up where her sister would have been. "I'll help you out around here Patricia. If my sister wasn't locked up she would be here. Trudy refused to bring Jake to see his parents incarcerated. I will let her know what happened if she ain't already seen it on the news."

Keke comes walking in the house and sees strangers sitting at the dining room table with her mother. Keke noticed that Pat was crying. "Mom what's going on? Who are these people?" Aunt Sarah gets up from the table to introduce herself. "Hi, I'm your Aunt Sarah. Your father's aunt." Keke looked at her sideways. "Mom?" Pat continues to cry before blurring out.

"Your Daddy is dead! He's gone!" Keke looks at everyone and leaves the dining room. The phone rings. Simone answers it. "Hello…no comment."

"Who was it?" Pat asked.

"Some reporter." She shrugged her shoulders.

Oh great this is just want I need to be in paper or on the news! Pat unplugged the phones. Pat went upstairs to the girls room the twins were also in there sitting on the floor watching the Disney Channel. "Mommy is Daddy dead?" JJ asked. Pat's face balled up immediately. "Yes. I was coming to talk y'all about this but it happened so fast…" Pat begins to cry with the twins and Tiffany hugs Pat tight. Keke remains on her bed watching television.

February 8, 1997

Jake's Funeral

The Fire Department paid for everything which was a big relief for Pat. Pat gave her husband a closed casket funeral. Around the casket were blown up pictures of Jake as a child playing football, a teenager hugged up with Pat, and of course pictures of him with his children. Pat gave the news false information so that they wouldn't be posted outside of Jake's funeral. She was so depressed about losing the love of her life. If it wasn't for Aunt Sarah and Tiffany helping out with the twins she herself would want to die. The phone calls and pop up visits overwhelmed Pat and the children. Keke started back up with her rebellious behavior. She had only been home once since Jake's untimely death.

It took the entire household to get Pat out of bed to attend Jake's funeral. Aunt Sarah dressed the boys in all black suits.

Tiffany wore a long black skirt with a black button up shirt. Mark attended the funeral with Tiffany, Aunt Pat said it was okay for him to ride in the limousine with them. That gave Tiffany comfort, she had been running around the house with the twins and going to school. The upside was Aunt Sarah started teaching Tiffany how to cook.

The entire funeral home was packed with love and support, well almost. Tiffany spotted Brenda sitting in the back grinning. What the fuck is she smiling about? Is all that kept running across Tiffany's mind. The twins sat next to their mother hugging and kissing her. Keke came in with some corny looking dude, Tiffany thought. He wore a Coogi sweater and baggy jeans with tan timberlands. She didn't ride in the limo with us. She walked over to the closed casket with crocodile tears in her eyes holding her ugly boyfriend's hand. Tiffany sat and watched with disgust at her cousin's disrespect. They sat on the other side of the room.

At the burial Brenda walked up to Pat and hugged her. "Now what are you gonna do? You like me now..." and she walks away. Pat tried not to allow Brenda's words to get to her. But they did. What am I gonna do? I haven't had a job since high school! Jake's checks are only going to cover so much. He didn't take out a large insurance policy. Tiffany whispers to Pat "What did Brenda say to you?" Pat just shook her head.

The repass was at the house. Tiffany, Aunt Sarah, and Simone cooked. Tiffany was so thankful for Aunt Sarah teaching her how to cook. Aunt Pat didn't have patience for it. Tiffany baked the chicken and helped with the sides. Janelle came over to the house but she didn't want to be at the funeral. The house was packed with people that Pat wasn't even sure if Jake met them while he was alive. Derrick came up with Vanessa for the repass also. Vanessa was very happy with her new family. Mark took the twins in the backyard to play basketball on their toddler version court. "Come on youngins!

I'm gonna show how to ball!" Mark tells the twins. The twins despite the tragedy had been in good spirits. Everything was neutral, no drama, just family and friends being there for Pat during her time of need. Mabel didn't come up for the funeral but she has called to check on Pat. "Burying a husband is not easy Patricia."

After the Repass

Tiffany, Mark, and Janell cleaned up the house for Pat. Pat and Sarah stayed upstairs in Pat's room having a heart to heart. "What are you going to do about that daughter of yours? Tiffany told me that she was pregnant and Jake made her get an abortion."

Pat pulls the covers over her face. I don't feel like this right now but I know it's a problem, Pat sighs in her thoughts. "I know Auntie. She didn't even come back to the house. If she comes back home then I have to deal with her. Either she's in or out."

"I tell her she's out. Let her see what it's like out there. She needs to learn a lesson coming to my nephew's funeral being disrespectful. She blessed my sister is locked up cause Claire would set a fire on that ass!" Pat couldn't help but laugh. Now she understands where Jake gets it from. "You right Auntie. I just never thought it would come to this."

"Child listen I've been there. I'll be back in the morning to see the twins and you. Get some rest Pat." Aunt Sarah opens the door to Tiffany eavesdropping. "May I help you?" She asked Tiffany who had the dumb face from being caught. "I was just checking on y'all. I'm gonna put the twins in the tub soon. Mark is going home and his Uncle left this card. Can Janell stay over?"

"Yes she can stay put the card on the nightstand. Thank you." Pat rolled back over.

"See y'all in the morning." Aunt Sarah goes downstairs to leave.

Jay A.K.A
Little John

"Jay is wild yo! This last murder we did was too much! We burned down three houses. Word on the street is that one of the fire dudes died!" Rambo, a new recruit, is expressing his concerns to Hazel. Hazel is counting her money at her desk. She looks up at Rambo. "Nigga is you scared? You know the rules in or out! Out means R.I.P no witnesses. If Jay was here hearing you bitch you would be dead!"

"Look no disrespect I just wasn't ready for all that. I'm in....I'm in. Niggas is just shook!"

"Naw nigga you shook! You sure you up to this soldier shit?"

"I'm in Hazel. I heard you stopped him from burning a house down though."

"I get Jay...you feel me? Stop asking so many questions...get ya soft ass back to work."

Hazel goes back to counting her money and admiring her long French manicure nails.

She finished counting the money up to make her meeting with Jay. Since the merger with Trigger some independents had tried to come up but failed. They didn't know that Jay was backing Trigger. The independents took Triggers presence as a threat to Southwest because he's from North. Leo and his crew found out the hard way and as a result three houses burned down and Jake's life was ended. Word is getting around that Jay is Satan himself. No other independents have tried to cross Jay.

Tommy and Buffalo are independents in South Philly but they are starting to get curious about Jay's crew. Jay started staying in South Philly to study Tommy and Buffalo. He thought he saw Keke with them. Naw can't be. Jay thought about making an appearance to Tiffany and Keke awhile back but decided against it. Finding out his fire killed his uncle has caused Jay some pain. He had to live with that pain forever. No one in the crew knew that.

Jay was wondering should he continue with the fires. Jay figured he would go at Tommy and Buffalo another way. Jay decided to wait a little longer. He understood the importance of patience. That's why Trigger was still in the mix. Trigger actually wasn't a bad partner. Next week Jay was going to meet his connection. Hazel was turning out to be the best right hand to have for a bitch. Niggas is starting to know not to fuck with them. Jay just had to figure out Tommy and Buffalo. He knew that they were cousins. They get their supply from Jersey. Still small time dealers and possibly pimps. Jay sent Hazel to follow Buffalo one night and it led her to a house on Hicks Street. She was able to get in because the bouncer at the door thought she was a hoe for the night. Inside she saw a pole in the living room and naked girls all over the house. Just as many niggas as girls were present. Orgies in the basement of the house. Hazel reported to Jay that the only two who had not indulged in any of the party were Tommy and Buffalo.

"They seem too stupid to start a war so they might be trying to partner up." Jay explains to Hazel.

Hazel passes Jay the blunt as they stake out on Buffalo again. "Yeah I think so too. So you wanna stay on them?"

"Yup. For awhile."

"Am I going with you to meet Triggers connect?"

"Still thinking about it."

"We kill him after we find out who his connection is right?"

"Chill Hazel! Hahaha! You are just as wild as me. How's the new soldiers?"

"They are cool. I'm gonna keep Rambo close."

"Why?"

"Tryna see something."

Jay and Hazel continue to share a blunt and watch how many people come in and out of the Hicks Street house. Jay notices a girl again who resembles Keke. She is walking up to the house with Tommy. What the fuck is going on? Jay doesn't want Hazel to know that Keke is his cousin so he plays it cool. "Look at this shit." He points to Keke. "Yeah what about her?"

"She looks like a high school kind of jawn. You said that trains get run up in there?"

"Yeah I saw her in there last time. She wasn't fuckin' she was sticking to ya boy Tommy."

"My boy? You funny Haze!"

Jay felt relieved that Keke wasn't apart of the sex fest. Jay figured that Keke had fallen into some shit.

Tiffany

My life has changed drastically. My Aunt is not the same; she has lost her mind. Keke left and when she tried to come back Aunt Pat wasn't having it. They got into a fist fight! I had to keep the twins in my room away from all the blood. I can't believe Keke thought she could beat her mother. I feel like I'm at my old house living with Brenda. Aunt Pat stays in her room most of the day. Aunt Sarah comes over and helps me with the twins. All you smell is weed coming out of her room. She goes out and comes back with bottles of alcohol. I haven't been to see Mark in like two months. He's come down here to see me but it's not the same. I'm so horny and I don't know if Mark is holding out on me. A part of me doesn't think so. Mark hasn't called me all week, every time I call him they tell me Mark isn't there or the answer machine comes on. I'm not gonna let him play me again either. I love Mark I do but it's other niggas out here too.

Janelle is going to spend the night. That's the only fun I have. If she didn't come spend the night on the weekends I would be crazy. It's not like I can take the twins to the gallery with me. Those two boys are too much. Jason has become violent at school starting fights. Aunt Sarah had to go up to their school twice last week. Jake isn't as happy as he used to be, he cries for Uncle Jake at night. This shit is just too much!

Tiffany goes and sits outside Janell should be coming up the block soon. A few moments later she sees Janelle. "Aye Janell!" Janell walks up to the steps. She places her black backpack on the side of her. "Tiffany what are we gonna do? I wanna go see Mike my new boo from down South Philly!"

"Girl you stay with a new boo! Shit I know Mark is probably cheating. I haven't given him any in two months. I need some too! I don't know who is gonna watch the twins though."

"Shit their mom! We need to be out! It's nice out too."

Janell had a point. Tiffany and Janell go inside the house. The twins are downstairs in the living room watching television and eating cereal out the box. Tiffany went upstairs to Pat's room. She knocks on the door. "What?" Tiffany pauses before answering Pat back.

"Aunt Pat me and Janell wanna go out. I'm leaving the twins downstairs."

"Okay."

Tiffany ran down the stairs and signaled Janell to go out the door. Tiffany and Janell ran all the way to the trolley stop. Once they got on the trolley the two girls just started laughing. "Girl! I'm so happy to be out! I'm ready to go have some fun!" Janell nods her head. Janell asked Tiffany if she had heard anything from Keke. "Naw. I think it's her calling from a block number. Aunt Pat whooped her ass. She was crazy to swing on her! That ugly dude got her actin' crazy! I wanna see her though she did tell me where she was."

"Alright we can get Mike to take us, he got a car."

"How did you meet him?"

"Waiting on the bus that day you ain't go to school."

I have to stop being so sprung off Mark, Tiffany thought. I haven't had any side jawns. He could be playing me hard!

Mike introduces Tiffany to his brothers Tory and Buffalo. Buffalo is immediately drawn to Tiffany. "How are you doing cutie?" Buffalo asked Tiffany as he sat beside her.

"I'm good. You?"

"Happy to see you!"

"Please...anyway. Janell, you gonna ask them to take us to Keke?"

Buffalo looks at Tiffany "Keke? What does she look like?"

"Why?"

"Cause I know a Keke she goes with my cousin Tommy."

"Your cousin is Tommy? He's corny looking. You look way better!" Tiffany states and laughs. Buffalo is way better looking than Mark. I can tell he is muscular under his white tee shirt. He has big brown eyes and a sexy ass smile.

"He thinks he is shit! Yeah we can go by there."

"After I go holla at Mike upstairs about something okay Tiff. I be back." Janell and Mike go upstairs. Tory lights a blunt and offers it to Tiffany. Tiffany takes it, she takes one puff and passes it to Buffalo. Tiffany has only smoked one other time and it was with Keke when they stole Aunt Pat's nick bag.

Don't get too high you don't know them. "How old are you Tiffany?" Buffalo asked while hitting the blunt.

"I'm fourteen. I'll be fifteen in July. Why? Is ya real name Buffalo? How old are you?"

"I'm eighteen. My real name is Tyreek. You pretty Tiffany. I wanna see what's up with you."

Tiffany smiled. Janelle and Mike came downstairs. Mike seemed happy but Janell looked annoyed. "Alright we are about to go to Tommy house." Mike states.

Tiffany and Janell get in Mike's black Jeep. "This is nice." Tiffany whispers to Janell. Mike is blasting Power 99 on the radio. I'm glad I'm out of the house! Is all that runs across Tiffany's mind. Buffalo turns around to Tiffany and smiles. Damn he better stop with all that smiling! Janell whispers to Tiffany, "His sex was wack! But he got money and a car..." the girls giggle to themselves.

Once they arrived at Tommy house the steps were crowded with children and two females. Buffalo tells the fat girl to take the kids down to the park. The living room has all leather furniture, a big stereo system and toys everywhere. "Y'all sit down." Mike tells Tiffany and Janell.

"Yo! Keke! Come downstairs."

"Hold on."

Keke comes downstairs to see Tiffany and Janell sitting on the leather sofa.

"Hey what are y'all doing here?"

"We came to see you. Janell knows Mike."

Keke hugs Tiffany and Janell. "I was upstairs with Tommy and he was getting on my nerves." Keke rolls her eyes. Keke looks different to Tiffany. She looks almost like a grown woman. Keke has a long weave in her hair similar to the singer

Aaliyah. Her nails are done and Keke is even wearing red lipstick. I guess corny ass Tommy is taking good care of Keke. Tiffany looks at Keke's arm. "You got a tattoo?!?"

"Yeah Tommy's friend did it. You like it?"

"Yeah. You look good girl."

"I'm getting money and Tommy takes care of me."

Janell jumps into the conversation. "You getting money how?"

"I strip and make drops for my man."

Tiffany sat there thinking about what Keke just told her. How did she get in a club? Keke is only sixteen. That's why she looks all grown up, she's probably lying about her age. "How do you get into a club? You got a fake I.D.?"

"Naw, it's down at a house. It's like anything goes. I don't have to fuck nobody though. I give Tommy a percentage."

"A percentage?"

"Uh huh I make a lot of money too!"

"How much?" Janell asked. Keke twirls her weave in her finger and blows a bubble with her pink gum. "Well last night I made four hundred dollars. Then Tommy took his cut so I got two hundred. I make one hundred dollars for drops but Tommy doesn't take that money."

Janell and Tiffany stare at each other. I know how to dance but I don't know how to be a stripper! "Y'all want in?" Keke asked. Janell said yes without hesitation. Tiffany thought about it. "That means I gotta sneak out the house! Aunt Pat well ya mom she is crazy! I'm tired of taking care of your brothers."

"Move in with us. We got houses. You like Buffalo, I'm sure you can stay with him."

"Let me think about it."

"Shit I can start tonight! My moms a porn star. I have seen her in a couple of them too." Keke yells upstairs for Tommy. "Wassup boo?" Tommy yells.

"Come here!"

Tommy comes down the stairs. "Baby they wanna work." Tommy immediately smiles. "Yeah...cool." Tommy looks at Janell and Tiffany.

Tiffany gives Keke a dirty look. "I told you I would think about it!"

"Tiffany try it out tonight and see how you like it." Keke assures Tiffany.

"Y'all got a body! Tiffany..no disrespect Ke, Tiffany you got a bubble butt!"

Keke rolls her eyes and laughs. "Let's go upstairs and see what outfits y'all can fit."

Hicks Street

Keke managed to find Janell and Tiffany outfits. Keke did the girls hair and makeup. Buffalo took the girls to the nail salon. Janell had a long ponytail weave that Keke just fixed up. Tiffany's hair was in micro braids so Keke curled them up. Tiffany and Janell couldn't believe how they looked. The house was empty for now. The rest of the girls were upstairs changing. One girl gave Keke a dirty look. Keke didn't even acknowledge her. "That's Tommy's old girlfriend, Shar. She lives with us in the back room. She ain't the bottom no more."

"Bottom?" Tiffany asked. What the hell is Keke talking about? Keke ignored Tiffany and started talking to the fat girl they saw earlier on the steps with all the kids. "This Dee Dee, Tiff and Nell. She watches over us girls. Don't let her size fool you I seen her drop a nigga one night for getting out of line."

"Hey how y'all doing?"

"We're good." Janell answers. Tiffany couldn't help but watch all the girls get undressed. One girl had tattoos all over her body and her vagina pierced. The girl caught Tiffany staring and rolled her eyes. Keke had on a sheer short pink dress. "My name ain't Keke here it's Cherry. Y'all need to find some names." Keke left the room. "What the hell does she mean like some stage names? I wanna be Black." Tiffany couldn't help but laugh. "Black what?"

"Just Black. Shit is hot right?"

Tiffany shrugged her shoulders. It had to be at least ten girls in this room getting half naked or naked to make some money. "I gotta think about the name thing." A girl walks over to Tiffany and Janell. She looks exotic in Tiffany's mind. Tall light skin, hazel color eyes, long wavy black hair. "Excuse me do y'all got a light?" She asked. Tiffany was stunned by her beauty. Tiffany reaches in her purse that Keke gave her for a lighter. "Here you go beautiful!" The girl lights her black and mild and smiles at Tiffany. "Thank you, what is your name bubble butt?"

"Tiffany. You are?"

"Tara. My stripper name is Wild."

"I'm Black." Janell introduces herself since Tiffany looks to be in a love gaze.

"Hey Black. Y'all new huh? Don't worry you will get used to it. I roll with Buffalo."

"Okay. We met him today. You mess with him?" Janell asked.

"Naw! This is about money, girl." Tara winks at the girls and slaps Tiffany on the ass.

"Tiff you are so gay!" Janell laughs.

After finally getting dressed the girls go downstairs. Keke is the pole swinging around. Strippers are either getting lap dances or doing orgies. I can't believe what I'm seeing. I can't believe I'm in a place like this. I need money though. Little John hasn't left any money for me or if he did Aunt Pat must have spent it on whatever. A fat guy approaches Janell. "You working sexy?" Janell takes his hand and walks off. Tiffany posts up against the wall watching everything. Keke gets off the pole to grab Tiffany. "Come work the pole!" The DJ starts playing Sasha 'Kill the bitch' Tiffany decides to start crawling around the pole. A few guys noticed and began to watch her crawl and shake her bubble butt. Keke fades to the back and watches her cousin. Tiffany spreads her legs open wide, she rubs on her breast. She noticed that money was being thrown on her body. What to do next? Get up Tiffany! Tiffany gets up and continues to shake her ass. Jump on the pole Tiffany! Tiffany listens to her inner self, she jumps on the pole and slides down with her legs open. Tiffany's first time on the pole wasn't as bad as she thought. Tiffany started to feel a rush. She gave out several lap dances and hand jobs. I'm not whoring Tiffany tells herself.

Mike drove Tiffany and Janell back to his house. Time had gone by so fast Tiffany couldn't believe it was three in the morning. Keke rode home with Tommy and three other girls including Shar. Only Mike, Tory, and Buffalo lived in their house. Mike explained to Janell that he wasn't like Tommy. Tommy was a pimp with a stable. Keke was his bottom bitch. That time when Keke tried to come home was because Keke and Shar got into a fight. Keke thought Tommy would kick her out for fighting Shar. Tommy loved seeing two girls fight over him. Keke was crazy for Tommy. Tiffany doesn't see why. Buffalo however has Tiffany's heart throbbing. Buffalo is more of a drug dealer than a pimp. The girls he has working in the house pay him one flat fee and rest is theirs. He uses them for eyes and ears. Buffalo is interested in doing business with Jay and leaving Tommy. Tara told him she thought she saw Jay go inside the house, but wasn't sure. Tara noticed Hazel come to the party a few times. Everyone knows if you see Hazel, Jay isn't too far behind.

Buffalo came into the house around six to see Tiffany sleeping on the lazy boy. "Hey sexy wake up."

"What?"

"Why didn't you go sleep in the bed?"

"I didn't know I could."

"Yeah go take a shower and come to my room."

Tiffany went upstairs to the shower. As she was coming out the bathroom Buffalo was standing by his bedroom door with no shirt on. Tiffany got really excited. He signals for her to come to his room. Buffalo's room was nothing like Tiffany had ever seen. A king size bed, thick black carpet, and artwork hanging on the wall. Buffalo picked Tiffany up and placed her on the bed. They started kissing passionately, holding each other tight, and then pushing away to stare. Tiffany's heart felt like it was going to explode. Tiffany forgot all about the fact that she never went home or the consequences she may face later. None of it mattered to her. What Buffalo was giving her was exactly what she needed in her eyes. I never went slow before...Tiffany fell asleep in Buffalo's arms.

"Tiffany! You in there?" Janell is knocking on Buffalo's door. Tiffany moves from under Buffalo's arm. "Yeah."

"Girl get dressed so we can go home! Mike gonna drop us off at your house."

"Okay!" Tiffany gets up and starts looking on the pretty black carpet for her clothes. Buffalo notices she isn't in the bed anymore. "You leaving?"

"Yeah...I gotta get home and go to school tomorrow."

"Okay. I wanna see you again Tiffany. We can go out to eat. Have you ever been to Red Lobster?"

"No, I saw it on T.V. though."

"You gonna come back and work? I heard you did good. I'm not gonna charge you tonight. But my fee for my workers is fifty dollars."

"You would still charge me after what we did?"

"It's business. This right now is personal. Here's my cell. Call me later."

Tiffany takes the paper and shoves it in her pocket.

"Does Keke have a number?"

"Naw not really it's a house phone. That's how Tommy is...I can give you that hold on." Tiffany takes that number as well.

She went over to the bed to kiss Buffalo. Damn his lips feel good.

On the way back to Tiffany's house, Janell explained to Tiffany what she was doing at the Hick Street house. "Girl I made easy money! I had sex with three dudes they paid me one fifty a piece! Mike is cool with me doing that cause I'm working. I told him my mom is a porn star. He said he saw one of her porns ha!"

"I didn't fuck nobody. I don't think I'm going to do that. I didn't count my money yet."

"My mom ain't gonna notice what I'm doing and my plan is that I'm with you. You can say you with me so we straight every weekend we got this!"

"I'm down Janell. Just have not came up with a name."

"Hmmm what about Bubble Butt hahaha!!"

"Shut up Black feet!"

When Tiffany got inside the house it was quiet. Aunt Pat's van wasn't outside either. The house looked clean too. "I guess Aunt Pat cleaned up and went out." Tiffany went inside the dining room. There was a note on the table that reads: *Hey Tiffany the twins and I are gonna stay over Aunt Sarah's house until Tuesday. You can join us or stay home. Call 215-335-2886. I cleaned the house before we left so don't mess it up.*

Tiffany called Aunt Sarah's house immediately. "Hey Auntie! How is Aunt Pat? I meant to call sooner."

"Everything is okay. Are you gonna come here? I'm close to your school."

"No I'm okay by myself for tonight. I will come after school tomorrow. What's the address?"

Aunt Sarah gave Tiffany her address and hung up. Tiffany has gained both of her aunt's trust. The caller I.D. had no missed calls from Aunt Sarah number. She did see that Mark called her twice yesterday and today. "Mark called me back finally!" Tiffany shows Janell the caller I.D. "That's funny Tiffany. How was Buffalo in the bed? I know y'all was doing something."

"Girl I never went slow before. It felt good. His dick is way bigger than Marks too! He wants to take me to Red Lobster!"

"For real?"

"Yeah he gave me his cell phone number. Oh and Keke's house number."

"Mike is buying me a cell phone next week. I can't wait. Are you gonna call Mark back?"

"Yeah I mean that's still my man! I will call him after you leave."

"Tiffany do you think I'm pretty?"

"Yeah. You're my best friend, why wouldn't I?"

"Do you ever think of wanting to do it to me?"

"Huh? Why do you ask that?"

"Tiffany you look at girls like how you look at boys. Do you think of wanting to try girls?"

"I have thought about it a few times.

"I still want men Tiffany but if you want to I will."

"I still want men too! I love dick but I do think about trying girls."

May 1997

Brenda

Brenda found her way back to Robert. He wasn't easy to get in touch with since that night he saw his son. Robert tried to block that night out of his mind. That boy looked exactly like him when he was his age. Big and tall which trick people into thinking they are older. I can't believe Brenda never told me I had a son! Now she wants to get back together. She wants my coke I'm not stupid. Brenda is only good for sex. Especially when she's high off coke Robert thought.

Robert sat in the living room while Brenda was cooking in the kitchen. "You getting that ready for me baby!" Brenda yells referring to the cocaine. "Yeah. What are you cooking?"

"Spaghetti! It's almost done."

Brenda comes out with one plate of spaghetti. She gives the plate to Robert and takes out her lucky rolled up dollar and happily starts snorting up the coke. Robert watches her with disgust. "Brenda why didn't you tell me about the boy?" Aww shit he wants to fuck up my high! "Because Robert, okay? I mean shit I wasn't sure..." Robert goes back to eating his spaghetti. He notices that it's much quieter in the house. "I thought you had a little daughter? Where is she?"

"She went with her daddy. Your son he's been gone. That bitch Tiffany with my sister."

"All your kids are gone Brenda? Where's my son?"

"He was out in the street last I heard. Shit he disrespected me! You find his ass! Now let me enjoy my high and then suck your dick!"

Robert kept quiet but he was beginning to hate Brenda. He still loved her dick sucks.

After she was done snorting she gave him the best blow job he could ask for. "Now I need your help with something." Brenda states as she gets off her knees. Robert nods his head yes. "Have you seen Joy?"

"Joy? Yeah it's funny you say that...she was at the bar a couple weeks ago asking about you!"

"Oh really...what did she say?"

"She was talking to Jenny, the bartender asking if you were still locked up. She got a new job downtown too. At a bank. She said she was celebrating."

Brenda had a plan now. "Far as anybody knows I'm still locked up ya understand...that bitch got payback coming to her."

"I won't say nothing...you gonna suck my dick again?"

"You know it."

Brenda two weeks later...

For the past couple of weeks Brenda has been tracking Joy. She camped out in front of her house for two hours before figuring out her route to work. Brenda would follow Joy all the way to her new bank job. On the first day of Brenda's stalking she stayed downtown Joy's entire shift. Joy gets off at five every day. Her days off are Tuesday and Sunday. I'm gonna get this bitch. Then John is next. They will all pay for my brother's death.

Brenda's plan to kill Joy is all she had dreamed about since she started following her. Brenda went to a Islamic store and purchased an over garment and niqab that was all black. No one would be able to identify her. Joy takes the el train home at fifteenth street station. Brenda planned it out in her mind to push Joy into the tracks or stab her. Brenda was so caught up in her thoughts she almost forgot to lock her front door. It's four o' clock you got a date with Joy. Brenda changed into the alleyway around the corner from her house.

Brenda waits patiently for Joy to arrive at the station. She always waits for her train in the front which is perfect for Brenda. Brenda stayed towards the wall to watch Joy. Joy had gained weight and it looked good on her. Joy wasn't wearing a jacket. Joy stepped forward to check for the train. Brenda noticed a change in her position, the train must be coming. People began to gather around for the train. Brenda moves in quickly, she opens her switchblade. Brenda stabs Joy in the back and then pushes her as the train is coming on to the train tracks. People began to scream and run. Brenda walks off quickly into the crowd. Once she gets outside of the station she flags down a cab. That lying bitch is dead!

Tiffany

When Pat and Tiffany found out that Joy was murdered both of them knew Brenda had something to do with it. "Do you think she would try to kill me?" Tiffany asked Pat. "We can't put anything past her. She must have paid someone to kill Joy. Brenda ain't that damn smart." Pat hoped that wasn't her sister and that she paid someone to do the deed. Tiffany didn't know what to think. John was still not allowed to have visitors or write letters. Tiffany was worried about him. However working on the weekends for Buffalo has been paying off. Tiffany suspects that Pat isn't sharing Little John's money with her. Pat's been going out more bar hopping with some guy she met on the Internet. The twins spend more time with Aunt Sarah. Tiffany was happy that she wasn't the babysitter anymore. Tiffany was taking care of herself and she liked it that way. Far as Aunt Pat knows on the weekends she's with Janell.

Tiffany decided after school to go meet Mark at the Gallery. He was waiting for her at McDonalds, and on the table were a dozen roses. Oh here we go Tiffany thought rolling her eyes in her head. Tiffany sat down on the opposite side of Mark. Tiffany doesn't even look the same. She looks grown and sexy. Mark is excited to see Tiffany, he's impressed with her new look. "Wassup Boo! I miss you!" Mark hands Tiffany the flower. Tiffany places them in her backpack. "Thank you...well I have been working."

"Working where?"

"I can't tell you."

"So when are you gonna come over and spend time with me?"

"I'll see what I can do. I got a cell phone now too. Here's my number." Tiffany writes it on a napkin. Mark can't believe how Tiffany is just brushing him off. "Tiffany you don't want to eat?"

"Why are we always going to McDonald's? I want to go to restaurants and movies. I know you been playing me too you think I'm dumb! Call me when you grow up!" Tiffany gets up from the table and leaves Mark.

Buffalo takes me out to the movies and restaurants. He has a house and he just got a new car. What do I look like eating McDonald's with Mark's broke cheating ass! She thought as she stormed off.

Tiffany felt good walking away from Mark the way she did. She still loved him but he needed to come correct. Tiffany got on the Broad Street line to Buffalo's house. Tiffany still couldn't believe Joy was dead. The news said they had no suspects. Tiffany hasn't seen Brenda since Jake's funeral. They didn't even acknowledge each other but she remembered her whispering to Aunt Pat. Whatever she said made her uncomfortable.

When Tiffany arrived at Buffalo's house Janell was already there sitting on Mike's lap. Buffalo was sitting on the lazy boy smoking a blunt. He blew a kiss to Tiffany.

"We need to go to Tommy's house. Keke called but she ain't sound right." Mike tells Tiffany. "She didn't? Well let's go!" Everyone rode in Mike's Jeep. I hope it ain't no dumb shit. "Could you hear her on the phone?" Tiffany asked Janell. "Girl not really."

All the children sat outside with Dee Dee. "Dee what's going on?" Tiffany asked her. Dee Dee didn't say a word and she continued to smoke her cigarette. Tiffany burst into the house to see Keke sitting on the couch with a black eye. "What the fuck happened to you?"

"It's nothing I'm sorry for calling."

Mike and Buffalo looked at each other. "No this isn't nothing Keke! Who did it?" Shar comes down the stairs smirking, Tiffany immediately jumped in Shar's face. "She didn't do it Tiffany!"

"So what! You think something funny?" Tiffany grabbed Shar by the neck. "Chill Tiffany! Don't hurt her!" Buffalo pulls Tiffany off Shar. Tommy comes down the stairs to see what's going on. "What's going on?" Tommy asked nonchalantly.

"You tell us!" Mike answers.

"Keke and I just had a misunderstanding. Didn't we baby?"

"Yes Daddy. I'm sorry. I told y'all it's nothing! I'll see y'all at the house later." They all leave.

Tiffany is heated that her cousin is allowing herself to be abused by this corny ass nigga. "Buffalo, is she serious! I would beat the shit out of him! You hear me?"

"Tiffany, she allows it. All those girls allow it. He picks out messed up young girls. He's had Shar since she was fifteen. It's been like three years now. I heard he's working on a new girl and she's twelve!"

"What? Y'all gonna let him rape a twelve year old?"

"I don't know if he touched her. I just know I have seen her come around. Those four little kids that are with Dee Dee are his."

"I thought he was like twenty!"

"Tommy is twenty eight! His dad was a pimp this is all he knows. But I got a plan though babe. I'm meeting up with the big man himself."

"Who?"

"Girl, you don't know who runs these streets? I'm meeting with Jay tonight! I want you to come with me."

Tiffany felt important for Buffalo to want me with while doing business is big.

Later on that night...

Buffalo and Tiffany didn't go to the Hicks Street house. Mike and Tory dropped off Janell at the house. All of them wanted to be present to finally meet Jay. The meeting was at a tire shop in North Philly. Tiffany was nervous when she saw two pit bulls chained up by the garage. Who the fuck is this Jay? Is he some kind of a psychopath? Why are we meeting him in this type of place? Rambo directed them to the back where Jay was waiting. When they walked into the office Hazel was standing by Jay with a silver pistol. Tiffany couldn't believe her eyes. Jay was my fuckin brother!

The Author

Porsche Day was born and raised in Philadelphia. Porsche developed a love for writing as a child. Her writing has allowed her to build a career as an erotic poet named "Thick Nubian Goddess".

The Diary Of A Former Sex Addict, is the first of many hot releases from Day. Day entrepreneur journey has her fearlessly pursuing acting while building her holistic coaching business.

www.ingramcontent.com/pod-product-compliance
Lightning Source LLC
Chambersburg PA
CBHW070754270326
41927CB00010B/2134